WHERE THE MIND DWELLS

SALVATION

John T. Eber Sr.

MANAGING EDITOR

A publication of

Eber & Wein Publishing

Pennsylvania

Where the Mind Dwells: Salvation
Copyright © 2016 by Eber & Wein Publishing as a compilation.

Library of Congress
Cataloging in Publication Data

ISBN 978-1-60880-489-4

Proudly manufactured in the United States of America by

Eber & Wein Publishing
Pennsylvania

A Note from the Editor . . .

A little kingdom I possess
  Where thoughts and feelings dwell,
And very hard I find the task
  Of governing it well.

—Louisa May Alcott
from "My Kingdom"

Welcome, poets and readers, to our next beloved volume of poetry, where "the mind can weave itself warmly in the cocoon of its own thoughts and dwell a hermit anywhere" (in James Russell Lowell's words). This is a safe place to share your thoughts, announce your successes, and grieve your losses with kindred spirits. Approach these pages as a meditative act, one that requires your focus and patience but will bring you peace and enlightenment.

Poetry is made of the mind-stuff on which you dwell, the ideas that run circles in your head; writing—specifically poetry—allows you to release those nagging thoughts, whether positive or negative. Feeling down? Or maybe you're bursting with emotions: Get a small notebook—or just a single sheet of paper!—and start writing. Not only is journaling a great mental release and path to inner harmony, it's a warehouse for all your writing ideas. At any time you please, you can walk down the aisles of your past thoughts, selecting those that cry out for development. That's your next poem, and we can't wait to read the polished draft!

We lean on inspiration to fire our machines of creation, but seasoned writers know the necessity of discipline. Committed writing is a physical practice, one that requires exhaustive training, continuous dedication, reflecting on results, and staying abreast of emerging trends. Amateur writers can also benefit from even a small amount of discipline. Start by writing a little bit each day, maybe with your morning coffee.

Another easy way to improve your writing is to read more. You will absorb more than just plot; you'll become more familiar with proper grammar, capitalization and punctuation without even realizing it. You'll be exposed to different sentence structures and will surely find inspiration for your own work. As Samuel Taylor Coleridge wrote, "Advice is like snow; the softer it falls the longer it dwells upon and the deeper it sinks into the mind." So give your mind the chance to sink deeper.

While poetry writing can be a studious practice, it's also a spiritual practice with an intimate transaction between writer and reader, speaker and audience, and corporeal and ethereal, but firstly between writer and self. We think of writers as performers for an audience, but before the artist shows off her masterpiece, she first nurtures the seed within herself. Wrap yourself in creature comforts, get out your favorite pen and notepad, and start releasing your cocooned verse. Together, we go forward into our own "little kingdoms" of thought, and there we shall dwell until meeting again between the covers of a book.

Desiree Halkyer
Editor

Greed

Once the seed gets planted towards oneself everything is slanted.
Few are happy with what is fair, they want more than their share.
They want yours and mine and whatever else they can find.
It is the cause for war so everyone else's they can score.
That is what the fighting is for because they always want more.
Once they have all that's in their town they start to look around.
They want the next county but it's never enough bounty.
If they can't have the whole state it would be a terrible fate.
Next is the whole nation but it's a short lived elation.
When Illuminati have endless sums of revenue what else can they do?
Then is power and control but it's not enough for the expanding ego.

The pair are so entwined just as grapes on the vine.
With these they create their exclusive wine.
Greed's all around, no bounds, hardly a selfless person can be found.
No need to look far and wide, only look inside.
If you can't find it inside first you'll never end your search.
You will only want more and can never seem to even the score.
It will always be out there but you'll never find where.
It will be when I have this but satisfaction will still be amiss.
Then it will be that but what you really need is sitting under your hat.
The best things in life are free, no need for terrible deeds.
Find your own gifts that are uniquely yours and give it away
   because you'll always have more.
The thing to ask yourself about greed is: "How much do I
   really need?"

Glen W. Gilbow
Odessa, TX

Inspiration for "Greed" came from events leading to the 2008 world economy collapse. Greed is the greatest threat to mankind. It's time for the world's majority to unite and disempower the greedy politicians and their puppeteers who profit from war, famine, shortages, and bankruptcy, which they create. The world needs a mass Gandhi movement so the money machine grinds to a halt. Let us not wait until there is yet more power and control over our lives and we literally have nothing left to lose.

A Long-Winded Preacher

The preacher went on and on,
Because he had a lot to say.
The congregation began to doze,
Some even began to pray.

It was in the hottest part of summer,
The air conditioner was on the blink.
Everyone was getting very restless,
With the sweat, armpits began to stink.

His sermon was about booze,
In the river it should be dumped.
"Shall We Gather at the River,"
The closing song, everyone was stumped.

A lot of hot air this preacher had,
He just didn't know when to quit.
But then his throat was getting sore,
Harder and harder to preach, bit by bit.

Finally, he said in conclusion,
"Now, my brothers, what more can I say?"
One member said, "Amen, brother,
Now, close, and let us be on our way."

James B. Ritter
Mt. Carroll, IL

Many of us have heard long-winded preachers and like to avoid them. I just wanted to give a humorous poetic viewpoint to describe them. It is my hope that you readers will get a laugh out of it—especially those of you who are those "long-winded" preachers!

The Pillow Fight

I never knew loving you would be like a pillow fight,
challenging each other from the start,
you knew from jump what I was about.
Of course I hid my feathers,
my pain, my past, my tears, damn I hid my soul.
That first hit caught me off guard,
there went the past.
We rustle around on the bed and I catch you,
laughing softy, that was your head.
You try hard to get me to open up but I'm guarded,
tickling me until I cry, the pain,
as a small amount of feathers fell out the pillow.
Jumping, ranting, chasing each other for clarity of what's
being held back,
two smacks and you fall.
My pillow burst spilling my tears and my soul,
you pull me close, hugged me, and told me, "I know."
How did you know that our pillow fight would make me…
How did you get me to…
How did you know?

Ladise Mangum
Harrisburg, PA

Mumbet

In shackles no more —
Her real name Elizabeth, but was called Mumbet
The colonel no longer owns her
All day working, working,
But someday, she was free
Her red badge of courage still there,
But just a remnant of her slave life —
Now she is free — free
Heart pounding, sun shining, free
Thunder, lightning, the storm of cruelty
But it will not block the path to freedom
Because she will be free, free
Heart pounding, sun shining, free
She toiled, she struggled
Almost, almost gave up
But she did not
Mumbet
Free
Heart pounding
Sun shining
Free

Andrew Shi
Herndon, VA

Fear the Barrack

Dark, gloomy barracks is
Where fight meet
Can you stand in spite of retreat?
You can't see the youngster
Near the monster
Thus his power on the
Mighty tower
When they go out of fear
They still need the use of gear
So, when the time comes
Life will one day be
Like drums
The barracks are a station
Of will and the act of drill
From that comes the
Conclusion
The fact of a delusion

Nevis Devulyte
Mt Kisco, NY

Cigarettes, Saints, and Sinners

They say those who don't sin are saints who paint others'
Hearts with gold
Their names written in bold on scrolls
Warming the cold hearts of the sinners
Can these saints really be trusted?
I saw a man who claimed to be a saint
His voice faint and fingers jet black
While smearing them onto the hearts of the fallen
I hear them calling my name
They only do this for fame
I came into this world not knowing I had to choose who to follow
These saints are not truly pure of heart
The man who I saw, had blood covering his hands from
Those who had fallen
That's when it hits me
Some try and disguise themselves as
Pure to harm the rest
This world is a cigarette
Filled with toxins and all we tar,
Yet we inhale each other
And wonder why we are not happy
I'd rather choose to love and help heal the wounded
Than to be called a saint who isn't one
I'd rather be called a sinner who tried to help
The rest because in the end
We all die as sinners

Natalye Michelle Salazar
Parsippany, NJ

Homecoming

My world was misty;
I felt so lost and confused.
I took a trip to change my world,
not knowing what else to do.
It changed my life for sure,
that trip more than twenty years ago.
It changed my life and made it good,
but the past began calling my name.
I tried to come home to yesterday,
but the past has no memory of me.
Now I am stuck in limbo,
unsure of who I should be.
I heard stories of the road not taken,
so I decided to check it out.
I liked it fine, it was good for a time,
but now I can't go home.

Candace Jean Mosier-McHenry
Bloomsburg, PA

Through the Meadow

Walking through the meadow
past the creek

Lead the way alone of
promises to keep

Feel a glance or two

Empowered by every
intuition, impulse bathed in
our love's repetition

Natalie E. Santiago
Homestead, FL

They Will Not Be Forgotten

Hell on earth
Outcast from society, deemed the inferior race
Lives lost, men, women, and even children
Old and young, strong and weak, sent to
Concentration camps like Auschwitz or Treblinka
All because of one man's views
Unbelievable, what people can do
Six million Jews killed, eleven million victims
Time will pass, but they will not be forgotten

Ruth Mendez
Hialeah, FL

Vanity

Visually stunning
All who see fall in love
But ever so cunning
The beauty is above
Never touch
Or pay the price
Forever in evils' clutch
Vanity the vice

Theresa Stull
Miami, FL

Darkness

Darkness surrounds her
She tries to stay calm,
But inside she is numb
Excellence awaits her,
But time escapes her
Her four walls cave,
As she is no longer brave
You ask her to stay,
Beg,
Plead,
But all she wants is to run away

Shannon Marie Giambanco
Selden, NY

Mirrors

Reflections
You mirror the image of the light in me
See my heart gives even when this world takes
Like the leaves from an autumn tree
You magnify all that I can be
So that the warmth of the sun's/son's rays can be felt
On imperfections on the surface of my skin
There comes a high,
When you highlight the light that shines from within their smiles
We are scarred and polished souls soaking in your unwavering love,
Looking for hope
Yet you see beyond the image that everyone sees
Because you never cease to see through the window of my soul
The horizons to my shores
Constantly the ocean waves and crashes into my sand castles
Because you know that it's your kingdom come
Not my will that needs to be done
So I run and run until my problems run out
Before the land that I stand on
But really that doesn't always happen the way I picture it

Oscar Kamazima
Columbus, OH

As a poet, poetry has allowed me to turn my stories into vivid images through writing. With poetry I look to inspire others to be aware of the world around them and to open their eyes and hearts to change for the betterment of society through life-touching creative writing and heart-driven actions.

Somewhere Else

He turns and nods a goodbye
From a house that he rarely leaves
Nothing has turned out as he thought
He closes his door
And returns to his empty room
And dried paintbrushes
And empty canvases, promising of stories yet untold
His unexpected anguish rummaged through his head
Listening to his thoughts
Trying to hear them without speaking them
Thoughts that are wise but impure
Always hiding in his room
Always on the edge of beautiful darkness
A long sigh and a sip of whiskey
His paintbrush seems to recall his loss
Placing each detail upon the canvas
Never telling the untold stories that were promised
But revisiting the closing door again and again
Somewhere else

Howard Boling
Senatobia, MS

Freedom

It wasn't easy, my friend
Once I started, there was no end
Busting brick walls and cutting up pipes
Such a devious plan, and no one ever thought I was the type
These were painful days and no one ever cared
But after six long months, I was out of there!
The big, bright, blue moon shone down on me as I leapt
As I fled across the ground, a skip in my step
Like I said, it wasn't easy
Two fugitives just looking to live, just as we should
Pepper shakers in our pockets
We ran as far as we could
Eventually, we were found
Everything was wrecked
And that's when reality came into check

Noor Iqbal
Spring, TX

This poem is actually based off the story of the two prisoners who escaped from prison on June 6, 2015. On the day that one of them was caught, I wrote this poem, inspired by their half-baked ideas of escape. The line, "pepper shakers in our pockets," refers to how they stole basic kitchen staples from a trailer. Now, when I first started writing poetry, I usually wrote horror. I soon changed to incorporate my own feelings in my poems. I now write poetry that I, or even other people, feel emotion when read.

Good Night

Some nights will feel like silk.
The pressures will fade,
And your bones will heat as exhilaration rushes through your veins,
And you will shake under the bass of a song,
That soothes the vipers inside, no matter how few.

Some nights he will stick to your insides like an ailment,
Memories, that make you pull back from the notion of real love,
False moments you spit the poison of,
Poison that filled you with such fantasies,
And the notion will fade further.

Some nights will be good, smooth, easy.
Others will feel like sandpaper,
Grains of past and present itches,
Dragging along skin—peeling layers back,
Until you are raw.

But each night, unfailingly,
There will be a cloak of a crushed velvet blue so deep,
And just as in every feeling you've ever met,
Its depth will bring beauty and fear.
For the most prolifically messy thing,
A thing we all cannot resist yearning for,
Is what we find in the night sky,
Something we cannot touch,
A something that is in every love we wish to keep but cannot,
A piece of eternity.

Nina M. McKee
San Bruno, CA

I'm a sixteen-year-old girl from California. Like every teenager—like every person—I have experienced both beautiful and tragic nights, and that's what this poem is about: from the nights where your heart aches for an absentee, or for adventure, to the nights that feel perfect, incomparably so. I hope you like my work, and I hope you find something or someone you recognize in their words.

Enemy of My Soul

Oh enemy of my soul
Don't you understand?
You have already lost the war,
I belong to Christ
In Him I've grown

You attack with such a vengeance
Like you think you have a chance
But the more you attack
The more I pray

You attack with flaming areas
I raise my shield of faith
You lie to me but my belt of
Truth is secure

Every time you attack my character
You will encounter my breastplate
Of righteousness

I have all the armor of God on
Everyday

You are mistaken if you think
You can make me turn away
My hope is in Christ
And to Him I give glory

Cathryn Edelman
San Lorenzo, CA

Between the Blades of Grass You Are Missing

Night air like a silk glove shushing the cheek.
Sometimes I fit your hand inside to save me from

A hollow June. Laughter from the party next door
Severs the light, or maybe it's the shadows that trees let fall

Like their second selves, too much to bear alone in the dark.
I could lie among them, forgetting mine, but who would be left

Standing when you finally return? No matter how much
Memory I bite off my lips, your half-moon of matte lipstick

Always remains. Let's never empty our mouths of our names.
I write and rewrite yours into my skin. Please remember me.

Tom Kozlowski
Hillsborough, NJ

Tom Kozlowski is a senior at the College of New Jersey studying political science and English. His poem is inspired by Julia Cohen and Federico Garcia Lorca and owes its dedication to Kalyani Parwatkar.

Your Name Is

Your name is Grace
When I am suffering from sin
Your name is Peace
When anxious thoughts move in
Your name is Mercy
When I do wrong, and I know right
Your name is Love
When I am accepted in Your sight

Your name is Savior
When I think about the cross
Your name is Why God
When I suffer loss
Your name is Help God
When I cannot find another way
Your name is Holy Spirit
When I cannot find the words to pray

Your name is Healer
When alone I cannot fight the disease
Your name is Jesus
When I find you on my knees
You have many names
But the sweetest one of all
Is the silence of a heart
As into your loving arms, it falls

Kayleigh Brianna Coker
Franklin, GA

I Miss You

I would do
Absolutely anything for you,

But

You do not think
My words are sincere

Because I have
A writer's touch
And a poet's tongue

Yes, the mere thought of you,
Causes a pain so severe

Agony entwined with
Many shades of blue

Hues so light they could lift a man's
Plight
Or sink a man's
Night

Alexandra Ruth Looney
Sacramento, CA

The Way You Were

Hair of golden brown,
Flowing smoothly down
Face of slender beauty,
Crimson lightly touched the cheeks ever so slightly
Ever when you were slightly shy,
Ever when you were touched by a guy
Lips of light red passion pressed against the skin,
Felt of velvet rubbing past my chin,
Arms that hugged to bring me in close,
To bring me in away from a world seemingly filled with sin
Hands with fingers stemming of the softest touch slowly moving,
Moving back and forth caressing my skin while soothing my soul
Legs of long slim sensuousness tangled with mine to form vines,
Vines of human flesh impassioning the likes of every thickening vein,
With every caress, and with every move
Feet caught in the moment like a camera caught capturing a picture,
A picture of the details alerting the moment it is being caught in
This is the way I remember you were,
Standing still, looking past all objects surrounding me,
Seeming as if I am looking through the clouds to a world only I know
All senses stir with just a single blur,
Flashing back,
This is the way I remember you were!

Brian Thomas Bitzer
Greenfield, WI

No Reflection

Talking to my reflection in the mirror
As I start fading it's getting clearer
No longer sure which of us is the real me
Can't quite figure out just what it is I see
Which of us is the reflection?
Or is the image an imperfect correction?
Images flicker in and out
Copy opens mouth to shout
No sound can escape
Just a fuzzy shape
I am trapped behind glass and metal
The entirety as fragile as a flower petal
How will I ever be free?
When I'm not even sure just what it is I see?
How can I be sure which of us is me?
Why can't these questions just let me be?
I'm screaming at my reflection to let me go
Staring back at me she's whispering, "No"
Standing where once I stood I see myself turn away
Forced to copy I do the same, will do the same forever now and a day
Talking to an empty space
Hoping I'm not just a reflected face
Talking to my reflection outside the mirror
I started fading and she got clearer
Never been certain which one of us is me
But I'm finally certain of which one of us is free

Amber Bratton
Dorena, OR

The Dream

He walked into the courtyard, handsome and debonair
He looked up to the balcony and saw her sitting there
He asked the waiter, "Who is she, so lovely and so fair?"
"The lady is from England," and he led him to a chair

She felt her heart apounding as she looked upon his face
His eyes seemed to be dancing and his movements filled with grace
The music started playing by the caballeros there
And he raised his eyes and asked her, "To dance, would you care?"

Joan Elizabeth Revilla
Bayville, NJ

This poem was written after a dream I had, and it is what happened in the dream. I have since elongated it but know it would be too long to fit the requirements. I was born in England and came to America in 1960. I have written a variety of poems for my own enjoyment over the years. I self-published a children's Christmas tale three years ago called Robot Horse; *it's written in poetic form and it was illustrated. Many years ago, Eber & Wein published my poem called "Breeze." It was more of what I would call, a nugget. I did buy your poetry book then. Thank you for your encouragement.*

Art

Sometimes I think about the past
When my hair was thicker
My reflexes were quicker
And I could tolerate liquor
Then I think I'm somewhere in the middle
Between giving up
Giving in
Too hard to win
On a good day
When the air is moist
And I have a little extra time
I think about nothing at all
But the tolerance is small
And I often have to sneak out
So's to have time with me
Sometimes I think about the past
Like a looking glass
I'm there somewhere
Sitting beneath the trees
My foot perched on my knee
Nothing but a sketch book and me
Feeling so free

Kathleen E. M. Segura (The Organic Maid)
Quincy, MA

I am currently studying Italian language and culture. Through trade school I am formally trained as a commercial artist and graphic designer, but when I attended the Art Institute of Boston, I received my first A in creative writing; the librarian said my short stories were a visual painting with words. Another English teacher said I should be a writer and asked was English my first or second language? I laughed and said first, but inside I was embarrassed because I am a terrible speller and spell by sound not rule!

My Beautiful Hummingbird Friend

Every bird has to leave the nest,
Even a hummingbird.
This beautiful, unique bird, is the bird I'll miss the most.
I will miss, the way its feathers glistened in the sun,
The way, it would ride the air current during the summer sun.
I will miss, its nectarine beauty to the core of my heart,
In my life, this wonderful bird, will always have a part.
I realize, you cannot tame a wild bird,
But, play a life in its own turn.
Oh, how I will miss this magnificent creature,
Because freedom is its teacher.
Fly south my summer friend,
Please do not forget me in the end,
My beautiful hummingbird friend.

Natasha Lynne Scaife
Latrobe, PA

As Blood Drips from Her Fingertips

As blood drips from her fingertips
She remembers what led up to this moment
She was laid off once again before Christmas
She did not know how to buy gifts for her children

As blood drips from her fingertips
She looked at the slashes on her wrists
Now her husband could collect the insurance money
That was the only thing that ever made him happy

As blood drips from her fingertips
She remembers the yelling from her husband
Wanting her children to have a nice Christmas
Yelling because she enjoyed her laptop

As blood drips from her fingertips
She did not want to leave her children with such a horrible man
Their own father treating them like dirt
She had no choice

As blood drips from her fingertips
She did not want to leave them here
She only wanted the pain to stop
This was the only way

As blood drips from her fingertips
She hopes her children can forgive her
Darkness begins to surround her
She gently floats into the abyss

Angela Dawn Coulter
Hickory, NC

A Message of Thanks

From me to you,
A message with an attitude,
To give you many thanks and much gratitude,
For opening up my eyes and letting me see,
The person that I loved that was beating me.
You tore my heart and tortured my soul,
But now that I left you, I feel free and bold.
No more beating and no more name calling,
To make me feel worthless and make me feel like I'm falling.
"A new woman am I," of this I can say,
For I grow stronger with each passing day.
My soul is at peace and I've sewn up my heart,
For the day that I left you, I knew I was smart.
So goodbye to you, wherever you may be.
This is a message of thanks,
                                To you from me.

Alicia Perez
Bronx, NY

I decided to write my poem, called "A Message of Thanks," because my heart was broken by the man I once was in love with. In the beginning he was okay but then he changed on me through the years. Through the years, I became a battered wife of six years. God gave me the strength to escape with my life. Now I'm finally free from the man I once loved who had beaten me without a care and love. A new woman am I and I'm free finally.

My Love

Always in my thoughts forever in my prayers.
My life would not be worth living if you were never there.
You bring about a smile when entering a room.
You always warm my heart at just the sight of you.
My world was dark and lonely as ashes with no flame,
Until you, my one and only, first spoke my name.
I count my many blessings and thank the Lord above,
For sending me an angel to show me how to love.
I promise to always honor you with respect and honesty,
In hope that you will understand how much you mean to me.
I could travel all around this world and every language I could learn.
None of them has a word for how much you have touched my life
    and put to rest all my concerns.
I pray my love for guidance each and every day,
To be the best I can be in loving you each and every way.
As a husband, a partner, a best friend and lover too.
I pray for guidance that I will never fail this love I have for you.

Michael Jason Jones
Seymour, MO

This poem is dedicated to my love, Elizabeth, without whom I wouldn't know what true love and friendship really are.

The Horror of the Lovely Sorrow

Please, do not tell.
Concealed in me lies something that will free me.
Deep down—a painful sore in some hidden door.
My inner core is screaming, wishing to be dreaming.
It says kill me, but will you free me?

Vanishing as a shivering breeze in a deceased world—
You cannot see me, but can you feel me?

As if I was a melting flake fallen from the graceful heavens.
As if I was a drop of rain carrying a tear's pain.
As if I was a dead leaf with the need to breathe.

Once more the cold approached.
My heart covered in hell's black—
and I do not bother to come back.

Can you save me?
Or will you fail me?

Alexander Nikolai Wilson
Duluth, GA

Bullets Were Voices

When I was little I wondered
What were those noises I heard?
I mean, I knew they weren't nice 'cause my mom said, "Get out
   the window!"
I was scared.
Scared 'cause my idol wasn't there.
Scared 'cause my brother was out where the noises were,
Not knowing if he heard what I heard.
What if the noises were talking to him?
To me, those noises were voices—
With no choices.
But as I got older, I started talking to people I hated.
Of course I'm talking about the noises.
I said 'em. These bullets were illnesses. I spread 'em.
I sent that one nigga to Heaven. Yeah I caught a body
But only 'cause he had a shotty
And I was told by my mommy, "Keep your guard up."
And now I'm smart and tough,
But I don't tell nobody I murdered
'Cause they'll talk about me bad.
And words? They hurt worse.
Keep it a secret. You wouldn't believe it.
And it's okay. It's better if you don't.
All this guilt and it was for my brother. With hope,
I wait till the day that I cope
From hearing the voices.
So now I keep quiet, silent,
Looking at the pistol and who's behind it.
Instead of taking action I mute everything.
I'm married to music now. All we need is the wedding ring.

Victor Josue Colin
Chicago, IL

27

I'm Thankful

Lord, if you have a few minutes
could I take a little of your time?
I just want to tell you
some things I have on my mind.

I just want you to know
how thankful I am today
for all the many blessings
you have sent my way.

I'm thankful for my husband
and the love he brought into my life.
I love him more today
than when I became his wife.

I thank you for our two sons
and what it means to me
to be the wife and mother
of this most precious family.

I thank you for my sister and brother
and for their families too.
Thank you also for taking care of my loved ones
who are up in Heaven with you.

Lord, I know your time is precious
so I thank you for listening to me.
I just wanted to tell you how thankful I am
and that I always will be.

Jackie Houk
Murfreesboro, TN

The Tree

The curve of her limbs
The sway of her trunk
The lay of her leaves
The strength of her roots
She stands tall, proud
From such a small seed
Planted with love
Before the spring rains
Could wash her away
She will stand watch
For decades to come
Over the lands
Over the hands
That helped her grow
Into the beauty
She has become

Maggie Mae Carter
Chesapeake, VA

O Winged Thing

O plague, thee darkest hour
It comes upon you, you duck, you cower
Thy wings to spread the moonless night
Your shackles bind, and dig, sure, and tight
In the deepest chasm, you show your fangs
One's visions clear, thy bind, the same
Some two, some three, four and more
To see things pass, and come before
They bite, they sting, to show, to shame
You, the chosen, you, to blame
To run, to flee, no place to hide
You grip the ghosts, that do abide
The light you seek, you surely find
To slow the beast, a tortured mind
You seek the answer, to him above
It is a gift, was sent, of love
To ask the question, how can it be
His only answer, the love of thee

Jeffrey A. Purcell
Clarksville, TN

Drifter

In the still,
In the calm,
I stand alone.
Beaten by waves
Pushing to and fro.
Caught up in the sand,
I cannot go.
Eager for freedom
But I am slow.
In the still,
In the calm,
I stand alone.

Jeniffer Skoczen
Anthem, AZ

White

Last night I had a dream
I was standing in a room of white
There were no doors, no windows, no walls
There were no sounds, or people in sight

I walked towards nothing
Hoping that there'd be something to find
My walk turned into a sprint
And I carefully ran out of my mind

I screamed at the top of my lungs
But my voice refused to come out
And so I stood in my place nervously
Unable to hear my own desolate shouts

I was alone with my thoughts
In this never ending room of white
My own mind beat me to my knees
And it had driven me too weak to fight

I woke up from the dream panting,
Making sure my voice is loud and clear
And it terrified me to realize
That the thought of nothing is my greatest fear

Amen J. Al-Moamen
Dearborn Heights, MI

I am sixteen years old and I am the author of "White." During many restless nights, I would just lie on my bed staring at the desolate ceiling while my mind wandered around corners, finding thoughts that would've otherwise remained hidden. With my arm crossed behind my head, I let myself think about things ranging from the very large, like the universe and its mysteries, to the very small, like the way our minds work and interpret different things. But my greatest idea was putting it all on paper.

Time

The days go by slowly without you
Sometimes hours pass
And thoughts of you are absent
Then something simple occurs

A traffic light changes color
It stops me in my tracks
Sitting alone encased in metal and glass
I fall into a deep pit of emotion
Trying to capture our last moments

Me trying to commit you to memory
Your face
The feel of your skin
Your smell
Trying to make sense of your death

The light is green
The cars behind grow impatient
With my meandering and honk
I continue on my way
Until I remember you

Benita Eoppolo
Wilmington, DE

Closed Eyes to the Alhambra

The bamboos,
I gently turn them away from me
As I, a sinner,
Gaze and walk into the holy garden.
The pond of lilies,
I bow to the wavering stems in the water
The gentle roots medicine and a delicacy —
I cannot escape worldly thoughts.

As these traditional strings
Pluck away at the feathers of my life,
My pride and plumage slowly flutter off into the wind,
One by one.
But I am not hurt.
I look as the clear pond quivers and trickles —
Ah, I am sorry, for I bring pain.
Ah that lovely sound, that —
Beautiful, serenity.

The porch a wooden earth
That I bless and sully with my innocent footsteps.
My presence embraced, but I know,
I am not there.
And I will never be.

But
The bamboo reeds still whistle.

Yuna Kim
Chino Hills, CA

The Blue Sky

Blue as can be
Goes as far as the eye can see
Has no beginning and no end
Covered with clouds on every bend

Birds chirp and fly up there
While people look up and stare
Airplanes are up there too
Up high in the blue

Trees reach with their fingers to touch
Wispy clouds and such
While balloons float up, up, and away
Dropped by children every day

The sun shines bright
With its brilliant light
Illuminating the sky
Up high

Sometimes it cries
Up from the skies
Like tears on our faces
Rain pours, leaving traces

The moon shines
The dark night pines
For the oh so blue
Sky to come anew

Victoria Dinov
San Diego, CA

My name is Victoria Dinov and I'm thirteen years old. I live in San Diego, California, with my mom and dad. My poem, "The Blue Sky," was inspired, hence the title, by the sky. I've always been fascinated with the sky. Why is it blue? I wrote this poem on a road trip. I was having a major "writer's block" when I decided to go to my beloved topic, the sky. While I was writing, the words seemed to flow out of me. In about ten minutes, I had my complete poem, "The Blue Sky."

Sweet One

Sweet one —
You're the apple of my eye.
It warms my heart
To see you smile.

Your secret wishes
And heart's desire
I've beheld as
Jewels through fire.
Pure and true they will be —
As you leave your heart with me.

Fly, little sweet one, fly
By you I will stand beside.
No need to fear;
It's been much too long
Time to soar —
Through the clouds toward the sun.

Soar, little sweet one, soar,
Leaving every encumbrance behind.
Freedom's bliss will be your song —
Harmonies of everlasting kind.

Kimberly Miller
Ceres, NY

The Story That Hides

My notes, my words, my thoughts:
these dreams dancing and playing
to the rhythm of my soul.
Can you hear their beat?
Hear their flow?
Feel the notes as they spin, they weave,
they twirl, creating such harmony?
There's magic here,
magic of the purest form,
raw and inviting, a sensual calling
that begs to be heard.
It pulses with my heart
and begs to be free from my soul.
Oh, the power that it could wield,
the passion that could be felt,
but only if I dared—
dared to unleash
what's hidden within,
risked the temptation
like playing with sin.
It calls, it yells,
it bangs within my unconscious,
a silent cry for it to be heard,
to be told, to be felt:
the story that lies within,
the story that hides inside of me.

Christina Lynn Piercy
Fresno, CA

Ashley Jones

I've killed love before
Always nevermore

Sane shadowed light adored
Oneness so briefly explored

Grew my soul waxwing high
Assuring spiraling resign

For sorrow clings tight
Around love's blind eye

So if memories must commit
Be of light before I killed it

Randle Stinson Garner
Spring, TX

For the Love of a Dog

How wonderful it is when a dog decides to be
Part of your life, giving love you can see.

She has her desires like food, treats and a good run,
But what makes her happy is when you say, "Come!"

Her vocabulary expands as you teach new words
Responding when you say, "Outside," "toy" or "birds"!

Oh the joy she shows by just being near
And sitting together while rubbing her ear.

She somehow lets you know without any words to speak,
Her actions and looking eyes express what she seeks.

Her eyes show love when she looks at you
It's really amazing no matter what you do.

God, your gift of a dog is a wonderment, it's true.
Her unconditional love reminds us of You!

Colleen Lear Hosford
The Woodlands, TX

As the Day Begins

Early in the morning,
  As I walk my garden fair,
I bow my head in quietude
  And whisper words of prayer.

"Good morning, Lord, the day is Yours...
  Do with it what You will.
Please guide me with Your Spirit,
  Your errands to fulfill.

"People out there struggle
  With illness and with woes.
Help me be a blessing
  Especially to those...

"With greetings and some words of cheer
  To comfort and to see
If their needs are being met
  And how You would use me."

In my garden, as I view
  The flowers growing there,
I think of needs and blessings
  As I speak with God in prayer.

Carol Holekamp Stayton
Steilacoom, WA

Golden Mornings

I will always remember
waking up next to you,
with that special golden city light
that dances across the scape
of multi-colored buildings.
Peering out across the horizon
that splashes light on
a city that never sleeps,
your waking eyes hold proof
that there was peace
and there was rest.
New light comes forth,
through the curtains
and into your room.
I'll always remember that color
that associates me to you —
hues of orange, some reds
and golden yellow, with traces
of purples that set against the green.
Cityscapes and golden morning light
will always bring me back
to that place — to you.

Sarai Moore
Brooklyn, NY

The Power of Forgiveness

So someone hurt your feelings. They said something that was rude.
Maybe someone just left you hanging, and you felt a bit confused.
Did the one you love break your heart to the point of no return?
Did they shatter the trust, it took so very long for them to earn?
So what if someone bullied you, when you were a kid in school?
They humiliated you in front of the rest because you weren't "cool."
Maybe someone left you out, didn't include you in their plans,
or maybe a disgruntled neighbor built a fence upon your land.

When someone jumps in front of you in the long line at the store,
or a coworker takes credit for something you worked very hard for,
take a few deep breaths, and think things through before you act.
Remember what your mom always said, "You are better than that."
People are only human. Everyone makes mistakes, and there is
no set limit to how many they may make.

Set your anger aside. Remember forgiveness is the key.
Sometimes it's better to let things ride, to simply leave it be.
You'll feel better about yourself, for being so forgiving,
and others may see your positivity, and change their way of living.
The power of forgiveness is where happiness begins,
and arguing is a waste of time because no one truly wins.
By holding a grudge, you're only torturing yourself. Don't you see?
Passiveness is courageous, and forgiveness sets us free.

Jennifer Jane Neeley
West Columbia, SC

The Giants

Giants, slowly expanding into every region of our world,
filling up the vastness of space.
My eyes have seen everything of dust
and comprehended them all.
My stomach growled when the stars were not enough.
My mouth overflows,
filling every crevice between my teeth
and the valleys between my taste buds,
with words so, so sweet,
Yet my jaws are aching —
they cannot move fast enough
and my gums hold nothing now but bloody sockets,
the only relic of what once was.
But my chest:
my chest still smolders with the stench of smoke,
my ribs remember the fire that was,
the branding that once brought bitter ash
to their inner rims
instead of stale flattery.
My bones incarnadine still,
I am hollow as a fireplace is hollow,
a cavernous tomb for a beast hibernating,
the den of a deity forgotten.
When our thrones became plush graves
phantoms stole the crown;
this utopia we created
reflects only our decay.

Danny Mara
Rock Hill, SC

The Song of the Lost

Shadows
Pain
Icy cold
Tearing the life away
Needles
Piercing the heart
Running through the walls
Abandon
The fire inside
Burned out
The embers
Dying down
In the frozen heart's embrace
The darkness
Closing in
A veil
Still
Over the skin

Meredith Drake Turner
North Richland Hills, TX

Time

It's free, but can be wasted,
Very valuable, but used worthlessly.
It passes slowly, but goes by fast,
Freezes at the moment, but leaves the next.

What a wonderful thing, but taken for granted.
People miss it, but don't change it.
It allows great memories, but also bad dreams.
Time is my best friend, but my worst enemy.

Karsyn Harry
Wicksburg, AL

My name is Karsyn Harry, and I live in Southeastern Alabama. I am currently sixteen. I have a big, beautiful family consisting of both parents, a sister, a brother and the last addition, my partner-in-crime, Preston my nephew. What inspired me to write "Time" was knowing that I will be leaving soon for college, leaving everything I have ever known. Writing "Time" has given me the realization to enjoy every bit I have because at any minute you or the one you love will run out.

You Are My Light

Words can't describe
The friend that you are
You shine in the night
Like a bright northern star

The sun shines its light
On the earth every day
But with you not around
My life seems so gray

You're the light in my life
You show me the way
You guide all my steps
With your presence each day

Heather Potter
Clinton, IN

Not on Paper

Ours is not on paper.
There is no test to measure.
He speaks and I finish the sentence.

The look the same each time.
I tiptoe to the kitchen while he sleeps.
I scoop the coffee that starts his day.

No words.
The cigarette blurs his face,
And I pour the cup always near the brim.

Beds by me.
It's how we do it.
Clothes are washed his way.

Sweet, fresh smell of sheets.
He folds them the same each time.
French is to do it right.

The same chair.
Dinner for two.
The thank you is a glance.

Communion of two souls.
All we need.
Ours is not on paper.

James Marion Henley
Raleigh, NC

You're Gone

All I wish is to endlessly weep in sorrow,
Let all my emotions one by one fall with each and every passing tear,
As they cascade down my cheeks endlessly
Something similar to a waterfall,
But I cannot.
My tears have limitations,
Although my emotions are not so kind as they are endless.
They stream endlessly like a void,
With every new emotion I feel,
I fall deeper into the abyss, slowly being drowned by my emotions.
And once the emotions have taken their toll and I drift to sleep.
Yet the sleep is not peaceful,
With my emotions in utter anarchy,
My mind begins to feel the overstimulations of emotions,
It begins to bring forth harsher emotions,
Along with painful memories,
That had once brought a smile or laughter
But now bring unpleasant and agonizing heartaches.
As the hours ticked away while asleep,
I awaking to fresh tears, and more heartache,
But with the constant cycle, I become immune,
Now all that is left is but a small sting,
And a scar on my heart:
All because you're gone.

Sonja Mapuana Alohalani Collins
Reno, NV

I Need You to See

Please... just please
Look... just look

I need you to see
What I can't bear to say
The words that tear my mind apart
The things that tear my heart apart

I need you to see
That I need your help
I may not make it back this time
And I don't want to see the end

I need you to see
That I don't want to die
But the demons in my head
I can't hold them back alone

I need you to know
If worse should come to worst
I loved you
Even if you didn't see

So please... please...
Just look... look...

Tiara Vazquez
Inez, TX

Haunting My Mind

As I close my eyes tonight
I know that you will be my first sight
The pain in my heart will disappear
Only in the morning to once again be here
Because living your dreams
Is not always as easy as it seems
When my heart calls your name
And yours will never feel the same
I tell myself it will be the last time
Your face haunts my mind
I am proven wrong
When I hear your voice that appears as a song
If it were up to me
I would have left the thought of you lost at sea
I have no control
Resulting in my heart yearning to be whole
You got through the gates without a fight
The guard was too distracted by the sight
I read the warning label
Then proceeded to put it all out on the table
You would think I would learn
Yet every night I return
In an illusion where I meet your blue eyes
To a place you love me, even if all lies

Marissa Kailey McKee
Papillion, NE

American Dream

Soar proud and
       Courageously

To the American natives
As participants in this live event we experience as life
We must earn a living by laboring six days per week
Therefore, Americans
Let us educate ourselves to be qualified for good jobs
Here in the freedom land of equal opportunity
For "We the People" by law have the right to special
Privileges and fair judgment as citizens to help us
Obtain this ambitious goal

Hear me
O wavers of the Old Glory
The Star-Spangled Banner
My friends
To be born in the USA is a great blessing to any
Individual so
Take advantage of it by achieving
Our ultimate goal the "American Dream"

           The patriot

Lorenzo Wright
Orlando, FL

Mangled Wings

Weary of all the conjecture, the slants,
Belly full of trite and typical rants.
It's enough for the troubled, the broken,
Who have to amend it with so little spoken.
Die trying while you wait for the bomb;
Pray for the respite of happy and calm.
Fly out in euphoric bliss, dance of death,
On days it is torture to merely draw breath.
Eyes nearly close, tresses whirl in the breeze;
Touch my face, then graze my lips and appease.
We must embrace these things we abhor.
Rise up, rise up—
Mangled wings need to soar.

Kyrian Lyndon
Mineola, NY

*Mangled wings came to me when I was waiting for a traffic light to change.
I was standing on the corner, coming home from work, feeling discouraged,
among other things. I was reclaiming my life, after tragedy and illness. I
had taken the first step. By the time that light changed, I knew I could do
it. I knew that I would. And I did.*

Stand Out

I wasn't born to follow
My insides are not weak and hollow
Stand tall and be a leader
For I am young and eager

What does the future hold?
No one is ever told
Be loud, be proud
For I am always going to stand out from the crowd

Ryan Connor
Farmingville, NY

Stay the Course

Behind those blue eyes, a landscape so vast
A musical reflection winding through a narrow escape
That mirror you see, it just cannot be
Absolute beauty unseen yet explained with every magical note
Trudging a sacred path lined in character and consequence
Seeking a constant state of chosen faith and spiritual hunger
Following the chaotic sound that is common ground
Each casting shadow brightened by pure radiant truth
Strength and commitment collide with a bold breathtaking beat
My soul she does see with each vulnerable and weary key
Awakened and aloud, something fierce has begun

Melissa R. Metz
Portland, OR

The Burden of Strength

To watch your loved ones suffer,
That is true pain.
A young bouncing baby boy,
Who barely has his teeth,
Abused by his mother.
You watch your father wither,
At the thought of his suffering boy,
You watch as he grows sicker,
With every rising sun.
You watch your brother die,
Just a little bit inside,
As his innocence is ravaged,
And all he can do is cry.
You want to ease their pain,
But you cannot in any way,
So you conceal your thoughts,
Protected by a lock and key,
And you simply pull away.
And by trying to avoid hurting them,
They just end up hurt more,
But you can't show them your pain,
You can't show them your suffering.
Strength is a burden for none,
But for those who must stay strong for others.

Ariel Ana Rodriguez
Norwalk, CT

Time Travel

I took a walk through yesteryear,
To a time so long ago.
I wished to see what was there
That I missed, now that I finally know.
I walked through the halls of my old school,
Saw classmates I knew back when.
Some I only knew by name,
Some I didn't know then.

I looked around for a calendar,
I wanted to know the year.
I asked someone what year it was,
They looked at me so queer.
"The year, well you should know quite well,
It's nineteen-forty-nine."
I was glad to know I still had time,
To locate this friend of mine.

Among those who wandered the halls,
I found the one I sought.
His eyes briefly met with mine,
But he didn't give me a thought,
Just hurried ahead to his future,
And I, I hastened to mine.
Little I knew, so long ago,
That our lives would someday entwine.

Anita M. Spainhower
Sparta, TN

I published a poetry book, Sense and Sentiment, *and a novel,* Tennessee Transplantation. *I've written short stories for an upstate NY women's newspaper and edited books for two friends. After my late husband passed away, I was on MyLife website when a gentleman (that I recognized as an alumnus from high school) initiated contact. He didn't remember me. Long story short, we are now married. My poem, "Time Travel," was written when I imagined returning to those years to find him.*

Beautiful Soul

Painted by the brightness of the sky
Haunted by the darkness of the night
Just the thought of you gets me high
But hiding in the shadows is an evil, it's just out of sight
The feelings make my heart flutter
Full of uncontrollable emotion
Just a look or touch makes me shudder
The love you give is a sinful yet virtuous potion
I can see the passion deep in your soul
Sometimes so passionate that words are spit like venom
It's a beautiful loss of self control
To be lost in your beautiful soul

Rachal Williams
Omaha, NE

A Different Day

Softly you touched, I melted and shivered
Theft of my heart, as you whispered

The tenderness and kiss with inquisitive desire
Now intensely covets as you spark a fire

That began in the night in the illuminations just off Broad
I left shining, prayers answered from God

Elated, renewed, unaccustomed delight
Captivated in a world of much excite

Subsequent moment, smothered my flame
Assurance lost, nevermore the same

Passion never ending, incomplete adieu
Conceivable wanting, trials a new

Ifs, wishes, what could have been
Another place, different time, just not then

Jennifer Wall
Greenbrier, TN

"Giants"

And there were *giants* then
In the days of our youth,
To provide, care for, and instruct,
Till growing; We too... became them.
And dying, they became *us*.

Sherman Atwood
Niagara Falls, NY

This poem is a result of my habit of condensing my thoughts as opposed to writing them in their entirety, which gets irksome! "Giants" is ambivalent and means "adults" or "men of genius" acknowledged growing up and also is a possible theory as to who "giants," referred to in theology, are.

From Seven to Heaven

There are seven seas that we can sail
Seven notes in the major scale
Seven stars that tell us where to go
Seven colors in the rainbow
A coincidence, well I think not
There are seven continents made of rock
And if you open up the book of wisdom
There are seven sins to be forgiven
So when looking for those gates to Heaven
Simply remember the number seven

Eric Carlson
Lago Vista, TX

being on purpose

being on purpose
think about it…
being
who you are
the radiant spark of perfect life
is effortless.
yet… that is your purpose.
you ask what is your purpose,
but the fact that you can ask such a phrase
encapsulates your purpose.
because you are;
you are worthy.
relax into this notion.
be with it.
meditate upon it.
breathe into it
and watch your life change.
open up,
communicate
love.
love yourself,
know yourself.
don't search your entire life
for something you already have…
you are your purpose.
let this truth rise within.

Nikki Lena Van Ekeren
Brooklyn, NY

My writing process consists of looking up and listening and then writing what I hear. I respect the flow of communication within and allow my poetry to emerge from a safe space and in its raw form. My desire to create a safe space for my soul is found within the words of my poems! When I was diagnosed and treated for sarcoma cancer in 2014, my soul attacked my body for immediate action. I wept. I questioned everything. I looked above and paused. Pressing pause on my life opened up a door inside… the door to my soul.

Love Is...

I once heard someone say that life is constant sacrifice
That we continually give up parts of ourselves to make others happy
But is this right?
Do we not only live once?
Isn't happiness the one goal that we all yearn to achieve?

Is it for gold that we strive? For power? For immortality?
No... Love makes us bend and break, laugh and cry, fight and lose
Love... a many-faceted word, like a priceless gem
Precious, indeed
But fleeting like the summer
Skittish as a wild horse
Afraid of being caged, afraid of being broken
Amazing to behold, but elusive in its capture

Treasure its beauty when it is found
Grip it tightly when it is yours
Fight fiercely when it is contested
Treat gently when it is safe

I once heard someone say that love is constant effort
That it must be nurtured with devotion, compromise, and tenderness
But isn't this true?
Do we not revel in its existence?
Is it not what poets have rejoiced in, and songs have highly praised?
I believe so

Claire DeConte
Moline, IL

Untitled

My pencil carves lines into the paper
Every line adds to the puzzle

A story is being told as I draw
A vision from deep in my head is laid out on the paper

Determined, I attempt to make my image come to life
Every inch of pencil mark counts at this point

The ideal picture is suddenly portrayed
My pencil roughly brushing various parts of the paper

After a long worth of time, my drawing becomes reality
I smile to myself knowing the amazing values of artwork

Alex Chimenti
Smithtown, NY

Grounded

I am dirt
I am the thimble full of earth
That keeps you tethered to this world
Of responsibility
Feet lodged in shallow soil
But mind, heart in the vapor
Of a white haze blowing away
To another time
Another life
You can't wait to get there
You said so yourself
How many trips around the sun
Did it take
For my buds to burst out from beneath
Your feet planted squarely on top
Of the earth restraining my vines
The leafy wisps pushed up on either side
In front and in back
And still you stepped out
Each time
Leaving a little more free space, centered
To be filled with blossoms

Janet Lorenzo
Los Osos, CA

Moon Cycles

It is dark, moist
I feel myself growing taller
Until suddenly I break through
A gritty substance
Light! Sounds! Warmth...
That I lean towards
Moon cycles pass as I grow
I am now tall and strong
Leafy greens are my hair
Families now live in my branches
I watch as the little ones grow
And leave the nest
As moon cycles pass
My leaves are ruby red, citrine, instead of emerald
Falling instead of growing
The families have left
And I am beginning to slow
My fox friends are burrowing
Preparing for the cold
As moon cycles pass
Cold, ice, snow now occupy my branches
Cutting to my very core
The warmth begins to drain from
Me and ones greater than I prepare to take my place
Darkness replaces the light as moon cycles pass

Madison Pollihan
Harrisburg, PA

Hey, I'm Fifteen

I am a bottle
Stored with rage
I am a princess
Filled with pain
I am the child
Who's buried beneath stones
I am a woman
Who wants to go home
I am an offspring
Made before marriage
I am the baby
Who died in the carriage
I am the girl
Who wanted less
I am the world
Locked in a mess
I am a patient
Never seen a doctor
I am a lock
Stuck on a locker
I am a fish
Caught in a net
I am the person
I will never forget

Kinsey Rebecca Scott
St. Louis Park, MN

Unrequited Love

I keep praying and hoping for the day,
when he will embrace me and tell me that everything will be okay.
But I know that day will never come,
because this is a problem that can only be conquered by one.
No this is it, I'm simply done.
My life is no longer fun and games.
I'm being haunted by a pain,
and I know I will never gain his love and affection,
and my heart is starting to convection.
It's as if I'm infected by a deadly disease,
I know you don't want me.
So go ahead and laugh,
as I cry over the fact that I've written your name in this book,
over a thousand times.
I've basically written novels about you,
and all the things that you do,
and you don't have a clue.
But I guess I'm the one to blame,
because I was the one who was so insane,
to call a pain like this love.
This wasn't a gift from up above.
I feel as I'm being shoved down a bottomless pit.
Or I've taken a billion hits,
all to my heart.
But that isn't the worst part.
Neglect washes over me from time to time,
and I thought the only thing that can heal me was poems
    that rhymed.
But the only thing that can heal me was just a little more time.

Aliah G. Ledesma
Newton, KS

The Respected Love

I held his hand close to my heart,
neglecting the hatred.
His eyes at first were unclear,
but soon enough everything made sense.

I knew he was only there for a certain reason,
because change occurs whether we like it or not.
Selfish one could say,
but it was my fault because I knew the path he wanted to take.

I played with my heart,
while he only used his brain.
His words were poisonous,
while I was speechless.

It comes down to destiny,
we met and we regret.
Your ways of love,
seemed as a heinous crime to me.

Simran Kaur Sahota
Vancouver, WA

Until the blood flows through my veins, my mouth will be able to speak. My speaking will float my ideas. My ideas will put strong words together. My words will be expressed through my passion, which is poetry. In fact, someday, it might be the career of my life if it is written in destiny. I definitely have taken a couple of steps to introduce my poetry amongst people. I am a local girl from Vancouver, WA. In the past year, I have published some of my poetry in a local Portland newspaper called Street Roots. *My favorite type of poetry is free verse. The poem "The Respected Love" is inspired from the good and bad deeds that have come up in my life. Indeed, my family is a major support when it comes to my poetry.*

She's Stronger

She's stronger than you
With her frail arms and petite figure,
With her pale skin and bold eyes,
With her plump lips and thin fingers.

People pity her, with her withered look
Of someone who's been thrown away
One too many times.
Oh, but don't be fooled
Because she's stronger than you.

She wakes up every morning
With courage seeping through her veins.
She faces her tormentors of many years
With a smile planted firmly on her face
And walks on:

Past the boys who hate her non-existent curves.
Past the girls who laugh at her lack of attention.
Past the teachers who scold her for her shyness.
They don't bother her.

They don't crush her strength.
They can't put fear in her eyes.
They dare not try to knock her down,
For she is stronger than them!

Hailie Michelle Hamilton
Grand Prairie, TX

Overindulgence of Love Narcotics

There are venomous substances that society forewarns us all about:

the distaste of heroin, the nausea of liquor, the delusions of acid,
and your parents disapproval of dating lady Cannabis.

But they do not caution you about the omen of love.
It is by far the most cynical and gruesome of all.
They warn you about the dangers of mixing drinks,
not about the dire catastrophes of a drunken Cupid.

They tell you to tread lightly with alcohol, but never inform you of
the underwater manifestation that reoccurs with every sip you take.
In result, a volcanic rupture of rancor is quietly waiting to flare
and burn every trickle of feeling you indulged in.

Rehab was not an option when the root of my habit was you.
A brochure wasn't given on how to get over you without withdrawals.
Nobody counseled me after my eyes could not bear the
brightness of the moonlight bleeding through my window.

How is it possible that you were my antidote and poison?
You condoned my drug abuse and reinforced it time and time again.
First, lavishly, then offering me loose change to get my next fix and
giving me enough so that I craved you endlessly when my
   high fleeted.

I guess pills aren't the antagonists in this novel;
maybe love is.

Raidys Rodriguez
Bronx, NY

*A person entered my life and made me feel magically alive at a time when I
was dazed and confused. I felt a whirlwind of unexpected emotions, and while
everything was positive in the beginning stages of our relationship, the tables
suddenly turned for the worse. I was unprepared for the darker side of love and
what became my first agonizing heartbreak. Love is the strongest narcotic out
there and if you allow it to consume your life, it is potent enough to empower you
or destroy you. Always love yourself first and others will follow.*

Breakups

You smelled like Sharpies and Windex
I've been trying to get the smell of you off my skin
I showered until my skin was red
and I've been scratching at my arms
'cause I can still feel your hands on me
but now you're just stuck under my fingernails
and I've been drinking mouthwash
'cause I can still remember the way your lips taste
but maybe I need something stronger
and I've been looking through my old notebooks
ripping out all the love poems about you
I don't want my books full of lies
and I've been wearing your old sweatshirts
they turned into my home away from home
and I've been getting' kind of homesick
but I'm also kind of sick of home
I could never find rest in you
being with you felt like being on a non-stop roller coaster
but the fun only lasts so long
before it turns back into fear

Amy Middleton
Mohegan Lake, NY

A Cliff

An edge of a cliff
A choice of a lifetime
Hold on… or let go…
Darkness all around
I can't see the ground
But the sky is no where in sight either

I hear my name called from below
The voice echoes as it says,
"Come, it's not so bad down here"
But then I hear a voice coming from above
It says clear and strong,
"Take my hand and I will help you up"
My fingers are slipping
My time is near
It would be so easy to just… let… go…

But suddenly I know
I want to live… to not let go
I don't want to see the bottom of this cliff
But I can't see the hand
The one that was offered
The one that promised to be there
My time is up and my fingers slip off
But I fling my hand into the sky I can't see
And the hand that promised to be there… caught me

Corabelle Tally
Salem, IN

Bee-Loved

I was yet a beatle or a beegee
A beachboy or bonjovi
Or whatever you call a juvenile bee
When something stirred abuzz inside me
At the sight of a full-blown beauty.

But where I hived she was
On the same ancestral tree
And I could not reach her
For she was close to the canopy.

In time my wings grew stronger
And I realized I had to fly over
And beyond the fence
To find my honey.

Le Badiable
Lakewood, WA

*I'm a natural-born Filipino citizen, a naturalized US citizen, and a senior
citizen. Call me a pun-ster or pun-ky — I'm cool, man — for I'm unrehab-
ably addicted to wordplay. I may not be young, but I can still cruise-control
at 70 MPH alongside a topless Impala. I may be old, but I am still quick
to road-rage behind a slow-moving broad Mercedes (no pun intended).*

Human Time

Human time converges
On a focal point.

Can the surgical precision
Be mastered to full attention?

Like a laser dancing
On the edge of a razor.

Hone in the entirety
Of your being.

Make that voyage from time's grasp
To know the timeless space.

Peer then, deep into the mirror.
See beyond the image reflected.

This wind and focus
Can finally be connected.

There is more to this human time
Beyond circle and line.

Take the challenge
And you will know the divine.

Atul Ranchod
Santa Paula, CA

Drought

The ruts
of smiles and frowns
crisscross my face
and spread out
at the corners of my lips
and eyes.

I am sucked dry,
a human landscape
at the end of a long year
without rain —
an unproductive land,
infertile and eroded by sorrow.

The road forward
is obscure and uncertain,
invisible in the blowing sand
of this dark hour.

Ann Coberley
Canyon, TX

*I live with my husband in West Texas, near the rim of Palo Duro Canyon,
and teach anthropology at Amarillo College. My poetry is often inspired by the
unique landscape around me but also by the circumstances of my life, good or
bad. "Drought" was the voice of a particularly difficult period in which I felt
powerless to act. Writing the poem was cathartic, as creative processes often are.*

Free

I'm a dandelion seed floating on the breeze.
I long to touch the ground so I can settle down and grow roots,
But I continue to float along instead,
A wish on the wind unfulfilled.
In a way, it's good because I'm always free.

Tricia Avenido
Van Nuys, CA

Missing

I feel a void in my soul
I feel empty, my soul is not loved
My soul has no feeling now it will always be empty
My heart is broken
I don't know when it will heal
The pain is strong and why
There's always something missing
He is gone so many years ago
I think that's what's missing
I let him go and now I will never know
What would have been so many years ago
Lately he's still here with me
So I know I am not alone

Carmela A. Bagnato
Jersey City, NJ

I Love You

The break in your heart, brings a tear to my eye.
I send a dart, but I hear you cry.
When you fell apart, I was standing with a pie.

I know it hurts now, but soon you will rise.
You may ask, how? I say, look to the skies.
Allow, him to compromise.

I'm here to help, with a helping hand.
You yelp, and demand.
But here I stand,
With a helping hand.

Amanda Hayley Purfield
Springfield, PA

I would like to say thank you to my loving family for all of their support. It means a lot. The inspiration for this poem came when my little sister and her boyfriend broke up. This poem was basically a letter to her saying life has its ups and downs, but I will always be here with my heart on a platter. This poem deconstructs the relationship between my sister and I, and as my mother always says, communication is key.

The Mural

I've not the brush to stroke the walls
nor the dream to add to this summer's scene
others have left their sketch
of sand, sea and rocky neck;
but I will not embark on ocean's dark
with a tide gone out

William Martin
West Roxbury, MA

Study Time

Unpleasant irony, it seems, haunts me again that
whenever I "study" not much progresses from where I began.
Distractions come by both frequent and sly,
and before I can stop it my mind wanders off,
like a thirsty horse to the nearest trough,
like a dog chasing a cat,
or the moth to the light,
like a bee to the pretty pink flower
or a bull to the fight.
Yes, that matador waves his red flag and entices me yet again,
to do everything, anything, except for that needy task at hand.

Gavin James Edward Hanson
Hayden, ID

Message from a Necromancer

Children
Hear the voice of my despair
They have pleased me
Sincerely
Their soul runs cold with the touch of uncertainty
And their mind strikes a vivid cord of bitter reality
Let them play the instrument of blasphemy
For they are my children of the dark

Men
Meet me in the hellfire realm
They have intoxicated their mind
Dine
As my legion against the refined
And their lust bring them to search and find
Let them drink their spirit out of my wine
For they are my men of the dark

Young and old
I care nonetheless
They follow my every need
Feed
I harvest the souls like one harvests seed
And they harken onto my words as I am who lead
Let them teach and let them read
For they are my followers in the times of Armageddon!

Cameron Joseph Beaty
Albuquerque, NM

Writing is the magic of the mind.

The Orange Globe

the orange globe
dipping into the sea
nary a sizzle that one might
sense there'd be
it then stretches its glow
across the horizon
lo and behold
in the a.m.
it starts all over again...

Joanne Brause
La Habra, CA

Him

Was it him the man she was so tempestuously in love with?
Was it, rather, him the soul?
Which filled every crevice of her neediness?
Which consumed her with desires as of yet never experienced?
Did she care to discern?

Karin Barga Napier
New Madison, OH

I Love You

I love you are words that are true
save those words for the person made for you
you'll know the person is true if they return the words to you
that person will stay by your side until the day you die
they will be happy when you are happy
sad when you are sad
and exited when you are exited
they will always remember your birthday
they will tell you about their day
and the words they will say day after day
are the words that you saved
the simple words, "I love you"

Emily Lindsey Chegwin
Winter Springs, FL

Thanks for Listening

Writers block soon as I open the notebook,
Untitled thoughts lost and blocked what my mental notes took.
My quotes shook up so I look up to the source it's my choice,
Show no remorse it was no forced hook up.
I'm too tough in the clutch to fall beneath my potential,
Like seconds left with no regrets I release the influential.
When's the last time you met the proper genius?
I see patterns to the madness, I'm here to break the sequence.
Ahead of my time a type of mind makes you wonder when God
    released it
Don't get jealous it's not only weather that dictates His new seasons.
So since I have arrived it's only right that I provide
Messages with return addresses only known beyond the skies.
While it fell through clouded vibes infected with earthly lives,
Somehow I can't deny my drive to open eyes,
To show you what I see within my current dreams
In attempt to set you free, though worldly chains have low visibility.

Joshua Miller
Raleigh, NC

What Man Will Never Know

Some things man should never know
Are things that God will never show
Man is too curious of nameless things
Of something that he can never attain

Heaven is far out of his reach
Perfection — the thing they all preach
Can never be found for their kind
This truth Heaven is trying to remind

He knows their minds will never be satisfied
God's own words were broken, yet ratified
He never gave consent or approval
Now man's own word has become so brutal

In God's name he calls on hatred
Saying we are sinners — never sacred
Judging every man except for himself
For *he* is right but not everyone else

And as his mind did grow
Man soon forgot God looks below
Perfection is *love*, and *love* alone
This is the thing man will never know

Danielle Blakley Sisson
Farmville, VA

Dancer

She's dancing by herself
across the stand
her audience the band
others watch and have to smile
as she twirls and glides with
such great style
she's lit up by the midnight stars
she's singing something soft and low
nods to the band
and they all know
the song she sings is not their tune
it's hers and it will not end soon
she sings of pleasant memories
things the rest of us can't see
and as she sings and dances near
the band stops playing
as she sheds a tear...

Robert V. Kaye
Powell, OH

Feel Fox Fold

I know I like the numb I feel
For feeling is emotion and I am bare.
My weeping colds
All ambition folds.
There is no grass to relax in,
No place like home.
Only this box
An abandon den,
Yet I'm the fox
Far from finish end.

Spencer George Morrissey
Morrisville, VT

Father

Forgiving when they stumble and fall
Accepting of the differences of each of his children
Tough when the time calls for it but with a gentle, loving hand
Humble in his achievements giving glory to God for them
     and passing that on to his children
Everlasting love for his children no matter where the path God
     has chosen takes them
Respected not for his rules, but for his humility and love that he
     freely shares and the guidance he shows them

Paulene Eskridge
Lincoln City, OR

I'm Never Far Away

They say getting a puppy is a countdown to sorrow
Predestined to plead for one more day
And though you feel your heart is breaking now
I'm never far away

I'll always be a part of you
I live inside your soul
So every time you think of me
Our two halves become a whole

And if you need me I'm still here
Surpassing all extremes
Just close your eyes and reach for me
You'll find me in your dreams

And when you think you'll drown in tears
Remember my brown eyes
And know I'm waiting here for you
A place with no good-byes

So you see, our story isn't ending
There's just a slight delay
But in the meantime, have no doubt
I'm never far away

Kathleen Thompson
Fredericksburg, VA

What the Heart Wants

My heart is like an open book,
so come on over to take a look.
I just want you to know,
that I need you so.

I have been waiting for you,
to come in and let me through.
I want you to see,
that this love is meant to be.

I have been waiting for so long,
it is as plain as a song.
The fact that I need you so much,
that I want to feel your touch.

I have been trying to let you know,
that I do not want to go slow.
I do not just want a friendship with you,
I want you to see me through life.

Dawn M. DiMartino
Edgewater, FL

You're Not Alone

You think that you aren't pretty,
The truth is, you don't see,
But I have something to tell you,
So, please, listen to me:

Beauty is on the inside,
Not just on the out
You are pretty on both sides,
So never have a doubt

You learn not to judge others,
But folks around us do
Lead not into the temptation,
Act like it's me and you,

Try to joke and get along,
Try to just have fun,
If you see something scary,
Don't be afraid to run

You need to live your life,
But you're never alone,
I promise I will be there,
To always guide you home

Shyanne Baker
Gwinn, MI

December 7

I remember this day
not because I was there
nor were any of my fore-bearers there
nor is there a song jingling in my head.

I remember this day
not because I am Japanese
nor Hawaiian nor in the Navy or Airforce
nor have I visited the sunken Arizona.

I remember this day because
back in fourth grade at the Canby 91 School,
the principal told us a story about a family
who gave up four sons to go fight the next day.

I remember this day because
I could never understand war, not really,
not the way politicians want us to understand it,
because even 9/11 feels cowardly in comparison.

I remember this day because
it would be unpatriotic not to,
because loss riddles the holidays
as we smile and sing through them.

Kerry Mohnike
Ben Lomond, CA

Rain

The rain falls on thirsty ground
And the air is filled with a scent
That cannot be described,
I sit and watch it fall
Remembering rainy days of times past.
A weathered barn
A loft of hay
Rain that beat a steady rhythm upon a metal roof,
Love so wrong, but so strong… it would not be denied.
The rain was falling on that dusty road that lay ahead
And fell behind
As I drove away, from you,
To watch the rain alone.
Now when I close my eyes I see you
Sitting in the swing
On the porch… listening to the rain
Falling steady upon the metal roof,
Alone.

Lynda C. Yeates
Deer Park, TX

Lynda C. Yeates has been writing poetry, songs, and stories for many years. Recently she became a published author of two novels and is working on a third. Lynda was born in the shadow of the Appalachians, and her poetry often reflects her memories of simpler times. Lynda now lives in Deer Park, a town near Houston, Texas. Lynda and her husband like to travel. They make trips to Ohio to visit family, including Lynda's mother and two sons. Creating is joyful; Lynda's desire is to share that joy with readers everywhere.

Bitter Poison

I have lived through pain
and desire nothing more than to escape
the feeling that I once knew,
yet I continue to pour my heart out
to a man who could care less about my condition,
a man who roams the earth searching for satisfaction
that I can never provide him.
I settle down into his cold burning stare
and feel the effects of love emanate from my bleeding heart.
Is this what love is supposed to be, or am I convinced
that I deserve nothing more than his charm?
He digs through me like a dagger,
pushing the blade deeper, deeper
into my bones which have become so frail,
until I have nothing left but an empty heart,
torn by the sharpness of his ego.
As pain drips down my chest,
I slowly drag my fingers through my own blood,
tasting the lust that was mistaken for love —
a deep bitter poison
which I willingly consumed,
a poison no doctor can get rid of.

Brittany Friedson
Monroe Township, NJ

Our Reality

Let me be your reality.
Let me hold you tight.
Let me take the nightmares,
If only for tonight.

Listen to my voice.
Let it ground your mind.
Feel me by your side;
You are safely intertwined.

You know me like no other.
You show me I can feel.
I am here to love you
And all that you conceal.

I am here to block those
That linger in your mind.
I am here to be your anchor,
To a peace of our own kind.

Selena Shandi Thomas
Mentor on the Lake, OH

Passenger Side, Front Seat

Passenger side, front seat,
It's where you both sat.
Passenger side, front seat,
Rattata tat tat, was the sound both guns made.
Passenger side, front seat,
Was your last seat before the grave.
Passenger side, front seat,
No one has been caught.
Passenger side, front seat,
Has the truth been straight out bought
Or sold to the highest bidder?
Passenger side, front seat,
From Vegas and LA news came.
Passenger side, front seat,
Life will never be the same.
Passenger side, front seat,
We all know Pac and Biggie,
But what about Little Sister?
She laid down in Oakland, California, one night
And Death it did not miss her.
Passenger side, front seat,
The bullets went through the front door.
Passenger side, front seat,
Did the bullets even the score?
Passenger side, front seat,
Does black on black go down smoother?
Passenger side, front seat,
Where was CNN and Anderson Cooper?

Robert Hadley Ulrich
Mill Valley, CA

Cancer

Like a thief in the night,
You came into our lives.
One minute we are able,
The next we are condemned.
Your methods are not restricted,
Your victims are not selective.
You are merciless and forbidding,
Callous and bold.
You take no prisoners,
Yet you leave us imprisoned.
You attack with no sympathy,
You leave lives in shambles,
Hearts forever shattered,
Words never articulated,
Families forever broken.
You are our adversary,
Yet never motivated.
You left us speechless,
But screaming till the end.
Screams of why!
Screams of help!
But our voices are just memories,
Left behind.
Those that have met you,
Will live to remember you.
Your name is unspoken,
But whispered in the lives
You have claimed —
Cancer.

Celine Meyong Krishack
Upper Marlboro, MD

Life Goes On

Life full of crime
So young, how could it be your time?
Only fourteen years old and at your waist is a nine.
Ready to take life at the drop of a dime.
But life goes on.

You're sixteen now
Your first baby is on the way
Seems like you were just a baby yesterday.
With the life you live will you be able to stay?
Your child may grow up without a dad some day.
But life goes on.

You're eighteen now
You and a guy scream and shout
You turn to run but then, *pow!*
Fall to your knees, your lights go dim now
Your two-year-old daughter is now a fatherless child.
But life goes on.

Did you fall victim to the streets?
Well, that is what it seems.
Feels like only yesterday you were a kid chasing a dream
All you ever wanted was to be a baller like Kareem.
But life goes on.

Shyanne Maye
Meridan, MS

View from the Backseat

As I look at the view from my rearview mirror as an adult,
I drift back to my childhood and my view from the backseat.
My view from the backseat was of highways leaving town
one highway after another. White lines, double lines,
yellow lines, ten, twenty, thirty, one hundred, a thousand,
one after the other taking me away from what I knew to
   the unknown.
Taking me away from my childhood friends never to see again and
taking me to my new best friends of limited time.
One line followed by the next taking me away
out of town and a life left behind viewed from the back seat.
I have counted many white lines in my life.
Counting the ones in front leading me
to my next new beginning and counting
the white lines behind taking me away from my old new beginning.
One town after the next and many white
lines, double lines and yellow lines
in between and viewed from the back seat.
Never knowing what's ahead
but always knowing what is left behind.
Now that I am an adult, I choose the highways of my life,
but as I look at the white lines in front of me,
I remember all the white lines behind me: ten, twenty, thirty,
one hundred, a thousand—all viewed from the backseat
always moving me forward.

Ruby M. Parks
Glendale, AZ

Paper Kisses

In an open book,
between the lines,
I find that I get lost in time.
When the cover closes and the pages kiss,
I discover, reality isn't something I have missed.

Ashley Cohagan Fleetwood
Spring, TX

Where's the Tortilla Soup?

My mother gave me pudding.
Where's the fun in that?
All I asked for Mother,
Was a can of tortilla soup.
Now she gives me donuts,
Well it's fine I say,
Though deep inside it's not right,
I was mad they say.
I run from my mother now,
I go to my basketball hoop.
She quickly runs to me,
She gives me tortilla soup.

Lena Suzanne James
Edmond, OK

Yellow, Sweet, and Sad

At the bottom of my cup,
where tea leaves once formed messages
foretelling the future
in days before tissue paper tea bags,
lies my yellow lemon wedge
with its pale buds of juice
like teardrops cowering in coarse, abused skin.
What message do these teardrops hold for me?
The flavor they impart is sour
mingled with the taste of sugary, amber brew,
bringing back long-forgotten nights
with good friends and happy, nostalgic songs
that left our hearts light and carefree.
How I love the taste,
the jubilance of this warm, wild juice,
a sunny, yellow remnant of the past.

Linda Klein
Los Angeles, CA

I am grateful to have my poem published here. I began writing poetry in high school, in an honors English class, at the age of sixteen. Three years ago, I joined a weekly poetry workshop for seniors. "Yellow, Sweet, and Sad" was written for the workshop, when we explored the use of color in poetry. It is the third poem I have had published out of three submissions. Being a tea drinker, I actually contemplated my used lemon wedge for inspiration. Just as there are method actors, I must be a method poet.

The Jealous Sea

The mention of her name is a riptide of emotion
Like a wave, my feelings crash down
I am frantic to keep my head above the raging water
My insecurities weighing me down

I am strong, I know I can breathe easy
Thoughts surrounding me but nothing to hold on to
I gasp for air, desperate to feel the sand below my feet
I see the horizon and the vast open water calms

The sound of your voice, the touch of your skin is my life jacket
I am buoyed back by the knowing embrace of the water
I float to the surface, the warmth of the sun touches my face
Panic is replaced with peace as I bask in the sea of your love

Maggie Sims
Redwood City, CA

This Woman

Heaven-sent
With a beauty that stops time
She intrigues me
My mind forever occupied

John Lesko
Auburn Hills, MI

Music of This Heart

The music of this heart flows light and kind
Slowly breezes with the wind
Through the small and quiet of the day
Permeates divine
Orchestrated in thy Lord's command

Ninette Carey
Middletown, NJ

A gift from God to hold me and keep me filled with his spirit: never surrender your dreams. I wake up everyday and walk, sail, write, dream, work, and love in that direction, not knowing my final outcome… but instead, enjoying who will hold my hand along the way… For that, I give my love… God bless!

Footprints in the Sand

Together we strolled, hand in hand
Leaving footprints in the sand!
Each wave came in with a sigh,
And took them away!

Jerald Christian Bangerter
Kaneohe, HI

Dear Lisp

Dear Lisp, you have caused years of low self-esteem
You have made me want to stop speaking
You have made me hate school presentations
But most of all you have caused years of embarrassment

Dear Lisp, because of you I have lost friends
Because of you I have felt socially awkward
Because of you I have felt extremely self-conscious

Dear Sister, thank you for standing by my side all these years
Dear Friend, thank you for making me forget I have a lisp
But most importantly,
Dear God, thank you for giving me the strength to live my life

Morgan Sick
Forney, TX

Rite of Passage

Drink the blackberry wine.
Kill the black goat.

Flat stone
Sharp knife
Full chalice
Blood.

Drink.
Kill.

Swallow, inhale
Slice, exhale
Feel nothing
Be nothing
Die.

I drank the blackberry wine.
I killed my black goat.

Kimberley Martin Stauffer
Lynchburg, VA

Change

If you change, the world will follow
With no transformation all there will be is sorrow
If you dream of a better place it will become what you are
Where you see no smog or skies the color of light tar
Where the world loves itself, and no one gets privy
A place that spins 'round and 'round and never gets dizzy
Any place where you set the example and live by it
Someplace where you are the unique purpose of change
A stop where you must be the change you wish to see in the world

Change where you make or become different
A chance for you to be non-belligerent
A way for you to become something for the world
A method to unfurl
In this transition from ourselves to the earth
We are not in trouble for even though we have ourselves a dearth
Let's say you change your nature
No one is needed to be denatured
A stop where you must be the change you wish to see in the world

Our world spins and swirls and it twirls
Making beautiful white pearls
The pearls are our people and the earth is our creator
So you see when you change, the world does too
A stop where you must be the change you wish to see in the world

Leena Prakhina
Glen Rock, NJ

Goodbye

Goodbye to all.
Today's the day. I've got to get going.
I'm on my way. I've wanted to die from day to day.
You've treated me right so don't take this the wrong way.
Stay in my heart and don't fade away.

Kody Lee Cannon
Great Bend, KS

Why Do the Clouds Cry?

Why do the clouds cry,
if the sun is still shining?
Is it the shaking fear,
that there is no silver lining?
Is it the dusty air,
dull, diminished, and grey?
Is it the blazing sun,
sometimes missing during day?
Is it the gloomy sky,
no longer bright and blue?
Or is it the knowing thought,
that you are up there too?

Lisa Marie Roy Furtado
Edison, NJ

A Melody of Peace

Today my heart sings, "A Melody of Peace,"
for the many who cannot sing this song,
for the many who long for joy and understanding,
and for those who hunger for the food of happiness.

They are the people of this world
seeking compassion, love and justice.
Can we but find in our hearts
the means to meet this global need?

Now a song of courage wells up
within those who see the way
for humanity to embrace each person
and act compassionately using this valiant determination.

And as more people bravely act
by caring, nurturing, feeding, loving,
and healing each other we can all cause our hearts
to sing in unity, "A Melody of Peace."

Brenda Kay Miller
Hoboken, NJ

I came from a family of four: Dad Robert Henry, Mom Esther June, Sister Vickie Jayne, and me, Brenda Kay Miller. Raised in Canton, OH, I now reside in Hoboken, NJ. This January 9, 2015, Mom passed away at ninety-one. Just after Mom's death, I had been thinking about "A Melody of Peace," a poem I had written a few years ago. She looked so beautifully peaceful with her lips slightly open as if she had just sung her own melody of peace. I offer "A Melody of Peace" for all who wish for peace and happiness throughout this planet, Earth.

Floating

Just simply floating through each day,
letting the winds carry me with monotony.
Apathy has taken a hold on my soul,
and has led me to numbness.
For the earth is endlessly spinning,
as my mind stays still.
A dormant Vesuvius awaiting eruption.

Kaitlyn Jayne Eagle
Harmony, PA

The Game

I swear your eyes were a candlelight
flickering towards my own personal oceans
and every piece of matter around us dribbled down to dust
because the things I'd be looking forward to were not nearly
as comparably stimulating as the game you and I had shared that day
and every other class period just like it
the ever so addicting routine of each of our eyes
doing more than just seeing but feeling
all the way across the room
playing the divertissement of who could glimpse
at one another without getting caught
and so far, we were both losing

Juliet Paige Norman
Tamarac, FL

Heaven-Sent Angel

I asked God in my despair for a loving woman who would care,
to be part of my life, and our love we would share.
An angel was sent, an answer to my prayer.
She set my heart free simply by loving me.
My love for her comes from my heart and soul
making me feel so complete and whole.
The passion we share is pure bliss.
We both feel it when we kiss.
There never seems to be anything amiss.
I hope it lasts forever; this is my wish.
Her love, I will always cherish
and in my heart it will never perish.
I never would have believed
a love like this could be conceived.
I long to hear her say, "I love you."
Sometimes I can see it in her eyes.
There are times when we're together
that it's hard for her to disguise.
Her gentle caress and her soft touch
melt my heart; I love her so much.
She is a woman true to her heart.
I only hope we never part.
In the beginning I came to befriend her
and now my heart can only surrender
to the loveliest woman I ever knew.
My angel, I love you.

Warren E. Taylor
Georgetown, DE

*I was inspired to write this poem by a woman who gave me unconditional love.
A friend in the beginning, Rhonda F. Timmons won my heart, and we have been
together, blissfully, for fifteen years. There is no end to our love.*

Five Types of Leadership

Type #1
You put aside everything just to help someone.
You care not what your job is; you do what needs to be done.
You show that other people matter more than they realize.
You disregard higher orders due to staying truthful.
Type #2
Nobody respects you, you feel so alone.
You are unsure what to do next, nor to whom to turn.
You decide to show the world that their opinions matter not.
You conquer your dreams, proving that nothing can stop
determination.
Type #3
You have the chance to grab a dream anyone would want,
Yet, it means to make someone change everything they hold dear.
You take a stand and decline, this offer that seems so grand.
You will not create your own happiness by stealing another's,
Especially when the other person does not realize what they may lose.
Type #4
Something embarrassing has occurred; you feel so ashamed,
Yet you look the person in the eye and admit your misdeed.
You choose not to avoid it; you take it like a man.
You learn from your mistakes, and acknowledge errors in your past.
Type #5
No one else is doing it, you are scared out of your mind,
Yet you know this must be done, so you stand alone.
You fight all fears and show that you will not be pressured.
You stand up for what you believe in, even against the entire world.

Dovid Nissan Roetter
Oak Park, MI

I have always been connected to the power of words, both written and oral. While my friends rushed out onto a sports field or court, I was one to slouch on the nearest couch with a good novel in one hand and a bag of chips in the other. I use writing to express my feelings and emotions or to simply remind myself of a life lesson I need to work on. This particular poem describes five members from my Birthright group who taught me the deeper meaning of leadership. Feel free to read my other writings at: www.asoulspeakstoyou.blogspot.com.

Trials

Can you remember when nothing went right,
When plans were derailed or money was tight,
With roadblocks in front of everything tried,
Then all your best efforts were thwarted or died.
If this has happened to you or a friend,
It's not the beginning of an unpopular trend.
It's only temporary, so endure it well,
You'll grow and progress, have this story to tell.
I remember overwhelmed and thrust into view,
Stressed to the limit and petrified too.
Once I was sick, it seemed to never cease,
I threw everything at it trying to appease.
This is a trial, being powerless and buffered,
To stop the experience our children have suffered.
Or caught in a story of accusations untrue,
And live the consequence with no hope of renew.
Someday I'll change my direction inside,
What remains is no detection of pride.
Then I'll have faith of the mustard seed,
And truly live honest, forsaking all greed.
Finally perspective my trials weren't in vain,
That life's experiences didn't drive me insane.
They prepared me intensely and made me strong,
To come off conqueror all the day long.

Jim Frank Wagley
Fort Worth, TX

A Cat's Tale

I'm a furry black cat named Midnight
And Halloween decorations in this yard
Don't scare me.
I'm rubbing my side against the wooden leg
Of a one-eyed pirate monster with a hook for a hand
And it doesn't scare me.
Now I'm prancing by a wart-covered, humped-back butler
Who is offering dead mice and bird innards to trick-or-treaters,
But it doesn't scare me.
I leap to the shoulders of a very large mummy
With blood-red blinking eyes
And it doesn't scare me.
My tail gets tangled in the tattered gray rags of a giant skeleton
But it doesn't scare me.
As I quietly approach the candy bowl
A screaming white ghost jumps out from behind a bush
And it does scare me...
I am still running down the street!

Patty Perreault Bennett
Lewes, DE

Christmas and Halloween were big time celebrations at my house. For both holidays, the decorations outside in the front yard were the most important part. We would set up all of our frightening life-sized Halloween figures on each side of the cement path leading to the front door, but one was always a real person who would scare the pants off trick or treaters. One day, recalling all of our "sidewalk monsters," I wrote "A Cat's Tale." To me poetry is a small amount of words describing big things. That's very powerful and the reason I like to write it so much.

The Ticking of the Clock

The ticking of the clock broke the silence,
as she waited throughout the long night.
She stared at the lights out the window,
praying with all of her might.

The man that she loved lay there resting
from the long day of struggles he'd won.
She knew that the struggles were futile,
and tomorrow just might be the one.

She held his hand and told him she loved him,
He smiled up at her, with his eyes blue.
For the long battle that he had been fighting,
would be over soon, this, now she knew.

The ticking of the clock broke the silence,
For the fight was over this time.
So take my love with you, she murmured.
In my heart you will always be mine.

Betty L. Allen
Sidney, OH

Death of Compassion

Flawed with betrayal,
imperfect behind walls of judgement
Aiding the slow unseen death of compassion.
Giving attention to the shoulder in
which stands the devil.

Seductive whispers of emotional
crimes caused unto others.
Forcing the painful swallowing of
our alibis.
An inexistent remorse for the heart
in which torn apart.
With each passing generation our
minds become more unstable.

More tragically impaired by the
poison we ingest.
Finding ourselves in a possessed
state.
Returning to a primitive form.
In time causing the extinction of
love and sanity.
Destroying all that was intended.

Travis Kruchinski
Scranton, PA

Wasteland

I myself am stitched together with imperfections
Like scribbled pen marks hiding mistakes
I by no means am close to the idea of who I should be
Or who I want to be
Overflowing with passions and ideas
Bursting with creativity
But suppressed by the cruelty of others
The tragic truth of the reality we all live in and have created
Continues to not impress me
It suffocates me like water in my lungs
The ignorance and disrespect of people ceases to surprise me
I battle myself and my mind, but no longer is my mind mine
It becomes a deteriorated mess
With ideas and information of which the media has created
I only think what they want me to
A brainwashing nonetheless
The struggle of heartache and the past haunt me each night
Creeping over me like a thief in the night
Coming to steal fragments of happiness
I've collected throughout the day
My heart and mind silently fall into an emptiness
Where it all collapses
Murdered by my own mind
Swallowed by the darkness
What a tragedy I force upon myself

Morgan Wallace
Nazareth, PA

Our Little Angel in Pink

You are free to skip among the flowers,
dance with the butterflies
fly with the wind, sing with the birds.
You are light as the feather from your angel wings.
Your halo sparkles in the sunlight like gold and silver glitter.
You can slide down a rainbow with the angels.
You are free to soar through the clouds.
Be free our little angel in pink.
We love our little angel in pink.

Shawna Ree Luckey
Rewey, WI

Beautiful, Beautiful

Beautiful, beautiful, such a lovely word,
but the word beautiful I think is absurd.
Beautiful, beautiful, what an awful thing.
Beautiful, beautiful, what torture it brings.
Beautiful should be someone nice on the inside.
Beautiful, beautiful, forever from it I shall hide.

Sara Dawidian
Las Vegas, NV

"Beautiful, Beautiful" is a poem that I wrote to inspire people to judge based on the inside rather than the outside. I hope that when people read it they'll get inspired to stand up to people that judge based on appearance rather than their personality, because it's what's on the inside that counts.

Unison

The moment is here, finally.
Nerves tingle, thoughts arise.
Immediately, they dissipate into
nothing; the sound of her breath,
her lips, focus attention on the
moment. Clawing at skin, we embrace,
sharing energy. This generates

heat, and thus, more passion. As I
slide my tongue into her mouth,
I taste her saliva, the ultimate aphrodisiac.
Attacks of deep breathing throw
me into a fit; I lean my head close to hers,
foreheads rest on each other. Energy rush-
es through my head into hers—wonderful.

I smell her hair—cocaine to me;
addiction begins with the loss of love,
and ends once one realizes it never left.
I lift my head to stare into her eyes, awe-struck
at the art of her soul; still holding our gaze, I
penetrate her—death of self,
resurrection of us.

Evan Larson
Waukesha, WI

Walking Home on a Foggy Evening

I watched the mist roll up the street last night
And fill the hollows in between the homes.
It muffled footsteps on the path and quite
Obscured the glowing lights of garden gnomes.
Where does the world go in those magic hours
When all the imps and will-o'-the-wisps abroad
Transform an avenue of leafy boughs
In shrouds of quicksilver and softly plod
The traces of the hoary air? Are all
The cares of the day extinguished like a lamp
Turned down against the lowering drowsy pall
Of sleep at day's end? These and others damp
My spirits but they cannot hide the glee
With which I turn around my front door key.

Michael Madill
Evanston, IL

Fateless

Running, racing, catching my breath
The sound of panting is reaching my death
Caught in fear brings everlasting tears
Save me for I am now facing a mirror
Sorrow, anguish, despair, is there no one out
   there who really cares?
Time passes as every moment flashes
Tick, tock to the song of sadness
Stars fall as each cast of darkness
Covers their light with madness
Save me now for I am about to take
The everlasting light, my fate

Katie E. White
Winter Springs, FL

Katie White was born and raised in Sunland, CA, as the youngest sister of the White family. While growing up, she spent most of her time writing short fictional stories, playing piano, and singing. When finances became an issue for her family, she obtained two scholarships and paid her way through college. After college, finances did not improve, and in order to afford a place of her own with her future husband, they both drove from California to Florida for a new beginning. Katie White wrote "Fateless" to represent her pain and sorrow dealing with people who gave her adversity, from elementary school all the way to the work force. Katie advises readers to take a step back and realize how their words and actions may cause hell and trauma in another person's life. In the end, is it worth treating people poorly? It may just be better to create smiles on other people's faces.

Journey's Flight

Angels of the night on
your journey's flight.

Stop and protect us
till morning light.

Be on your way with
your journey's flight

and come back to protect
us another night.

Theresa Magby
Ceres, CA

My Friend

I'd like to be the sort of friend that you have been to me…
I'd like to be the help that you are always glad to be
I'd like to mean as much to you each minute of the day,
As you have meant, *good friend of mine*, to me along the way…
And this is just to wish somehow that I could but repay,
A portion of the gladness that you've strewn along the way…
For could I have one wish today, that this only would it be,
I'd like to be the sort of *friend*, that you have been to me…

Tom Lech Jr.
Tampa, FL

Gone Too Soon

A precious gift tender and rare that is now in *God's* loving care,
With a heart of gold that was gentle and kind to all he knew
A gentle soul who cared that has gone too soon
For his body may be gone
But he remains in our hearts and soul
For there he shall remain as time passes on
Remember the times that were once shared and his dreams shall
   live on
Through the memories that were made
The people he encountered, the friends he made
And the loving family he leaves behind
May his soul rest easy as he opens
A new door as he is greeted by those whom have passed
As he is embraced by love once more
Although it saddened my heart to see him go
Perhaps God needed him more
We may never understand why he had to go
But I'll always keep those memories that we made
And good times we shared therefore
He'll never be far as his spirit lives on
For his presence shall always be there deep within my heart

Janice Theresa Casler
Union City, NJ

For My Parents, Thank You

Thank you to my wonderful parents, for my beautiful wedding day!
Thank you for everything you do for me, every single day!
When I was sick, you did everything to make me better:
chicken soup with my medication, and a nice big comfy sweater.
When I was sad, you did everything to make me smile:
favorite movies with some popcorn,
laying on the couch for awhile.
When I was curious, you would show me, we would explore:
Anne Frank's hideout, Big Ben and the Louvre! Who could
     want more?
You taught me about my heritage, that's really swell,
civil war reenactments, plantation trips, seen the liberty bell.
You taught me about your heritage, I can never be dull.
I speak English, et Français, y Español.
I've learned to be compassionate and caring, just like you.
I still donate clothes every year, and give those in need of food.
I was always top of the class, you are both great teachers;
a principal and a professor, I didn't stand a chance with either.
I've grown into the person, the young woman, that I am today,
with your wisdom and intellect leading the way.
Forty years you've been together, that is amazing, that is love.
We will follow your example, ending all disagreements with hugs.
Never giving up, always working as a team.
Relationships aren't always as easy as they seem.
Yet you have stuck it through and always given me the best.
Now our marriages are equal, thank you Supreme Court of the US!

Kathleena Mercedes Hurd
Brooklyn, NY

When the Supreme Court of the United States made its ruling on legalizing same sex marriage throughout the country, I was so overwhelmed with joy, I penned this piece almost immediately. It's more than a piece of paper. As a child my parents taught me that if one of them was ever to get really sick, the other would not be allowed in the hospital room because our family didn't have the same rights as others! That has always bothered me. I'm happy that my parents' forty-year relationship, four-year marriage, is now granted the respect it deserves.

Nesting

I am afraid to turn on my air conditioner.
For two years now,
Two little brown sparrows
Have built a nest
Underneath it on the window ledge.

I hear them come and go,
Their familiar flutter
Talon grab and beak bump.
I wonder what they hear of me?

We sometimes surprise each other
In unexpected sightings
Like yesterday
When
With a beak full of straw
One of them stopped short
As I,
Leaning over to pick up a book
Came beak to nose abruptly
Staring into respective eyes
Caught in the act of daily living
Feathering our nests
With nothing but a pane of glass
Between us.

Patricia Guerard
Portland, CT

Home

Why are you crying?
You shouldn't shed a tear,
Just because I'm not here
I'm still here close and near
Even though you can't have
My shoulder to cry on
I'll always be here for you to lean,
I'll listen when you talk
I may not answer from the start
We'll never be far apart,
Never lose your hope or faith
I may answer you a certain way
Even though I had to go
I feel no pain and no sorrow
It was time for me to move on
To my new home where I belong
Until we meet again
I want you to hold my heart in your hand
Hold it gently, hold it firm
For my heart can fill the world
My time has come for me to go
Where I'll wait for you to show
Home with me where we shall be
Together again gracefully...

Kurell Law
Garfield, NJ

The Seedling

A warm summer's breeze
caressed the last dandelion seed,
sending it swirling up and around as if it
were a tiny fairy
dancing up into the great
wide open.
Destination: "unknown."
As dusk fell upon the day
the seedling descended,
nestling down into the warm
earth, awaiting it's next rebirth.

Carol Gordon
Corinth, VT

Someone's Path to Happiness

I was bleeding, fast.
There was so much, and you saw every single drop of it.
But still, you sat there.
You sat there staring at the lines across my body,
with blood flowing out of the them,
with the biggest smile on your face.
Because my red blood, looked like red roses to you.
And the pain in my eyes, was your path to happiness.

Isabel Elder
Summerville, SC

The Gift of Life

Precious! Wholesome! Right from the start.
Gracious! Spectacular! Oh magnificent art.
You were made with such motivational chamber,
In you I see the world's greatest treasure.

Oh gift! Oh life! Such awesome formation,
So colorful! Diverse! Earth's vibrant companion.
With hands and feet you take great steps,
Like heads and shoulders you interconnect.

Who could have designed this magnificent art?
In whose splendor and beauty we cannot depart.
Oh what a gift that the giver should give,
For with this gift we were made to live.

This gift is given for all to use;
The young, the old, it's for you to choose.
Cherish it, mould it, let it work for you,
Live it, love it, it's the best thing to do.

Julliet Ann-Marie Miller
Mount Vernon, NY

Julliet Miller is a passionate writer. She writes poems, songs, music, and short stories. Her purpose for writing is to uplift, inspire, and motivate in a positive way. She wrote "The Gift of Life" because she believes that life is one of the greatest gifts on Earth.

I Am

What moves beneath my skin?
A beast sleeping, lying within?
A madman staring with a cynical grin?
I know not what I am.
A child left alone in a world unknown,
I could not see, as the dark surrounded me.
Though my eyes adjusted, to show me the truth.
Am I good? Am I bad?
Am I sane? Or am I mad?
I do not know, and suppose I never will.
I am what you need, though, you may not see.
The answer lies within, I am not what you want me to be.
Shall a hero be needed to all, a hero I'll be to prevent the fall.
But if a villain be needed as much, all will feel my sinister touch.
And if on occasion a madman be called, I will come to kill them all.

Stephen James
Mount Airy, MD

The Mask

Every morning of every day,
I put on a mask to hide myself away.
I wear a mask to hide my face,
To keep others from seeing what's underneath.
All the things which weigh me down,
Things which force my face to frown.
The mask shows the person I wish to be,
Someone who can be happy and carefree.
But eventually, even the mask cannot hide what lurks below.
Even the mask begins to show,
The things inside which I already know...
It is dangerous for people to see,
The person I've hidden inside of me.
Soon the mask begins to fade.
It dissipates and melts away.
Another mask must be made:
Another version of me,
Someone to become,
Someone to strive to be,
To hide the darkest parts of me,
That even I am too afraid to see.

John Vincent McGrann III
Ellicott City, MD

John McGrann is a senior at Howard High School and will turn eighteen in November. This is his first publication, and he is honored to be included in this collection. For him, writing has become a method to cope with feelings or situations when they become too much to handle. He hopes to reach out to others, who share these thoughts and emotions, to let them know they are not alone. To those who don't, he hopes to help them understand. Regardless of who reads this, he hopes for everyone to feel something real from his writing.

Lost Key

I told the demons to walk away,
but they told me they are here to stay.
I lack the voice to tell them anything.
I am a prisoner of my own mind, and I'm sick of it.
All of this and everything is not willing to comply,
to the voices that told me all these lies.
I've lost to the beast in my heart,
and he rips my insides apart.
Knowing this, I let my life fall apart.
Joy is a past memory that seems far away,
and those pearly gates seemingly don't exist.
The light that illuminates,
hope is dimming, and faith disappearing.
Make me feel like me once again.
The smiles that once implored,
a destination once explored, take me back.
Please, because there is nothing more.

Emmitt Joseph Pichardo
El Paso, TX

The Irony

Your love will be the death of me,
Yet, I've never felt so alive!
So go ahead and kill me...
We'll call it assisted suicide.

Paola Izamar Polanco
Fairburn, GA

Are You a Pumpkin?

Are you a pumpkin
or a sweet pea?
How 'bout a cutie pie as lovely as could be?
What about a little ham
or a buttercup?
I suppose if you don't answer,
I'll just eat you up!

Amy Bunting
Monona, IA

Amy Bunting is a proud wife, mom of three boys, and fifth-grade teacher. She enjoys reading and writing poetry to show as examples to her students and sons. Adding humor to everyday experiences and creating poems is a passion of hers. Inspiration for "Are You a Pumpkin?" came from her young sons and baking in the kitchen. Amy thought about how comical it is that children's nicknames are often connected to food.

Unseen Truth

The realms of truth go unheard,
because they are asphyxiated on their own verity.
The stretch for true life is far too distant
for the typical person to ever come across.
Their eyes are sealed from it all,
for ignorance has always been bliss.
To be as one, none are unique,
for in these days, it is made for all souls to be the same.

Jessica Nelson
Oakland, CA

Early Wonder

Golden blonde curls caress her young shoulders
While fixated blue eyes follow a bouquet of balloons
Across the foyer they bob up and down
Connected are varied hues of shimmering ribbon
Child's hands delightfully reach out to nab
Yet cannot untangle a single streamer
Frustrated tears pour from her wide, wistful eyes
A parent hears her cries and wraps secure arms around her
The whimpers lull away as a lilac balloon is freed from its nest
Giggles erupt when her new friend bops her mother's nose
French doors open and the family plus wonder go home

Serena Ruzbacki
Newcomb, NY

For Merita

She had many names in life;
Daughter, Sister, Mother, Wife.
Through all these and past her end,
My special name for her is
Friend!

Chessie Roberts
Newport News, VA

Losing Touch

I don't keep in touch.
I know I don't call.
I keep myself in a pouch.
Without you, I've always felt like I would fall.

I should be closer to you, this I know.
Not keeping in touch with you is low.
You mean the world to me.
It's hard to just let things be.

I'm afraid to get close for fear of losing you.
For all eternity, with all my being, I will always love you.

Chandra C. Bennington
Mt Pleasant, NC

A Moon in Darkness

In the tranquil forest, far far away
The birds chirped their melodic song
The moss grew damp and green
While the stream gently ran along

But I ran through the forest
Hands firmly in my ears
My vision blurred by sobbing eyes
I was ready to embrace my fears

When I turned around, I wasn't aghast
I saw above my head a crystal moon
Surrounded by darkness and emptiness
Why was it dark ever so soon?

The darkness made me content
But I was not pleased with the moon's allure
I looked for faults and flaws in the moon
Something that would make it not so pure

So I started counting
Each crater
Each uneven hill
Each traveling crack
Each time I have been hit
Each time they left behind a scar
A bruise that will never remit

Phillip Batov
Staten Island, NY

The Legacy

So quiet now with Dad and Mother gone.
My task today, to call the legatees,
in places past that once shaped their lives.
To each a small bequest, "in honor of…"

Expecting gratitude and platitudes
I call their alma mater, and explain —
thinking of the photo of them, so young
and earnest, in mortarboards, commencing.

Next the art museum: I remember us,
children amid the mummies and Monets.
A dignified voice (not Midwest) thanks me,
"So kind of them to leave bequests for art."

I call the hospital foundation next,
"Both doctors, he a surgeon, long ago…"
I give their names. A pause, and then she says,
"When I was a baby, he saved my life."

Alice Klippel Livdahl
Paxton, MA

My parents were both physicians, who practiced in Northwest Ohio for forty years, before retiring in Massachusetts twenty-five years ago to be near me. I always knew that their real legacies would be in the lives of their patients. Nonetheless I was deeply moved by the last call I made on the day I phoned the charities named in their wills to verify addresses. This poem tells that story. The lady in the last stanza is now forty-four years old.

Words Don't Compare to My Love

With all my heart I love you
No words good enough to explain
Thoughts of losing you my one true love
The crushing feeling of unbearable pain
You're laying in my arms dreaming
As I watch you sound asleep
Praying to God in the heavens above
That you're mine forever to keep
Knowing in my heart and soul
I've never done anything deserving of you
Know that in Heaven or Hell my love
There's nothing for you I wouldn't do
In my heart and soul I know
Together forever we are supposed to be
Two hearts bound together forever
The most perfect love our life's destiny
For an eternity I am yours
Even longer if I could
If loving you longer was possible
I promise you my love, I would
These words I've written for you
Still don't explain how I feel
Until the day that I met you
In my life, love wasn't real

Matthew Matteis
Wallingford, CT

It has been a very hard journey. For this first poem published, I would like to thank all those who have inspired me: my mother Sheryl who's always been there, my father who passed in 2011, and my sisters Nicole and Christine. I want to thank you all for your support, including my children Connor, Tessa and Ethan and especially my beautiful fiancée, Jenna, for whom this poem was written: I love you. Without you God knows where I'd be. To my beautiful fiancée, I love you with all my heart. You are so amazing, you are my most perfect dream come true.

Leaving Stockholm

Sensitivities put my young self at a disadvantage;
Maps went missing.
And while I was not naturally graceful,
"I'll kill you!" was easily caught.
My driver neglects to look in the rearview mirror.
Words lobbed like a dirt clod from the side of the road,
"If you know what's good for you...."
Fact is, I didn't.
Add a fist and the red flashing light couldn't convince me to go.
"Don't be so stupid, stupid!"
Silence behooved me, "Be a good girl."
Then it befriended me, "Tell and you're dead."
As fear is cornered and convinced it's love.
"I'll kill myself if you leave."
Empathy has done me a disservice.
How many times did I pass the exit?
A change of scenery does not necessarily change the scenario,
I heard every word, you see, patterns bound in belief.
Fast lane to 50, I found the road a while ago.
I'm a decent driver now, much to Mother's surprise.
The road markers of time now the faint yellow of a bruise,
As hope was unpredictably found in a foreign wayside,
A landscape so breathtaking that the dirt is all but obliterated.
Still the black tar bubbles in the heat and resurfaces.
God, point me back to the highway again and again,
That "most excellent way" out of Stockholm.

Kelly Keyser
Seattle, WA

Like a Spider

Like a spider brings one fear,
So does fear bring terror near.
But when forgotten, this creature of dread
Disappears to make its web.
A web that seldom can be seen
Until a light shines on its seam.
And like the spider's hidden art,
We hide with fear behind our heart,
Afraid of the terrors that life hath wrought
And forgetting to realize what we ought:
That maybe when fear is forgotten about
It turns into beauty we never should doubt.
A beauty so perfect, so lovely and special
That all fear once present lies inconsequential.
Secret and silent until the bright dawn
Streaks through the dark shadows, we stumble upon
The promise of happiness, yet first to get there
We had to be tormented, tested by fear.
So if we do not dare to seek
For that which is hidden, buried deep,
Then we are surely doomed to wait
For that dreaded spider to dissipate.
Never intending or hoping to find
What beauty is hidden behind fear's disguise.

Hannah Rose Berggren
Bergen, NY

My name is Hannah Rose. I am sixteen years old, and I am one of seven children. I love to write and eat pickles. My writings are extensions of the way I feel and perceive things, printed elegantly in attempt to give others a glimpse of what I see and of what I am. It's a piece of me for everyone to see, and I'm glad I found the opportunity to share it with more than just my family.

Untitled

I have nothing left.
I have nothing more to give,
Nothing more to say.
There is no breath in me that holds the energy to breathe.
My body is limp.
My emotions have run dry.
I cannot shout, I cannot speak, I cannot feel.
There is no hunger, no wanting.
There are no great desires.
I have nothing.
I hold nothing.
There is only void,
Nothingness.
I am naked in the dark.
But there is light,
Small, like a lamp on a foggy street.
At first it is dull... distant.
And then it becomes closer.
It becomes brighter.
It fills the air.
It fills my soul.
The light—it comes from the darkness.
It stands firm in the black void of time and space.
It fills the damp slumber of nothingness.
It heals.
I am bathed in light.

Lisa Marie Toal
Denver, CO

Immutable

"Oh—my beloved—with locks as crashing ocean waves,
And a heartfelt voice chiming as fate's guitar:
In beholding your face my heart caves,
With a peaceful love bound to prevail so, so far.

Your truthfully mature thoughts are quite zesty.
What a wonder it is that you are so sweet.
Using only words of humility—you care not to test me:
Happily imbibing the wisdom I lovingly secrete.

Your words are honeyed upon the morning's dew.
They trickle from your lips as the leaves of fall.
I scribe these words to openly declare to you,
That you are a marvel which shall not soon grow dull.

The very fact that you are now mine, is the silky balm,
Healing the coarseness of my lonely life without love.
"Us" forming into "I" is as the pen in the writer's palm:
A designed unity that creates a perfect work from above.

Do not always be with me as wild as the mustang,
But—by fortitude—cling tight even unto our final sunset.
Within this dwells a certain peace devoid of any clang,
As we become an immutable love story none easily forget."

Morgan C. Coudriet
Meadville, PA

*By the power and guidance of the Holy Spirit, this poem is one of my many
hopeful attempts to artistically display unto all people the infinite and awesome,
pure and true love that God has for man, through His one and only begotten
Son, my Lord and Savior Christ Jesus. The church is the bride of Christ. Every
Christian's duty is the great commission. I hope to perform this duty, through my
God-given artistic abilities. If you enjoy my poem, I gleefully ask you to read the
greatest true love story ever written: the holy Bible.*

A Written Apology to the Sonnet

I'm sad to report an injustice great,
to the regal, paramount poem lost.
I fear a needed atonement is late
to this faded influence we have tossed.
The grand ancient temples have given way
to great skyscrapers sparkling in the sun.
The framed mosaic did not have a say
and the melodious abstract has won.
But, as its memory stands, should we mourn?
Free-verse moves like falling rain to rivers
A unique fingerprint from whom it's born.
Diverse beauty in all it delivers.
To the Byzantine sonnet, in its hearse,
I'm sorry, but I do prefer free-verse.

Sarah Giardina
New Windsor, NY

Darkness

He was a shell of a man,
Half of what he could be.

A darkness had carved him out:
One that couldn't be shaken.

Sometimes he looked perfectly fine,
Other times his eyes appeared hollow.

The scariest part was no one took much notice.
He blended in;
I suppose that's exactly how he wanted it.
He didn't like questions,
And he desperately tried not to burden.

He carried the darkness all on his own.
It had been buried, and reburied
Over and over again.

He was stubborn if nothing else,
He would not let the darkness out.

It left him living, just barely.
He was living only in the sense that he drew breath.

Courtney Sweet
South Glens Falls, NY

As Angels Watched Overhead

A man is at work, a son of the South.
A woman is at work on the man at work, a daughter of the South.
What is his trade you may ask? Her trade?
Both honest trades, both born to create. Craftsmen at work.
Yes, we've stumbled upon craftsmen at work… as angels
    watched overhead.
Both work, as the spirit works through them.
She goes about her business with faith, and a knowing of the brush.
He tends to the wood, bending it to meet his needs.
While the man in the painting holds a skirt of wood,
She speaks the language of paint holding a brush of wood.
While we are but witnesses.
This man, this solitary man, meets his wood.
This woman, this solitary woman, meets her canvas.
Both suspended in time and space fashioning art from life,
Upon a solitary planet, beneath the stars of time.
They say art can soothe the soul,
Music lifts the spirit, both bringing everlasting life.
But first, wood must be fashioned, strings attached, paint mixed
    and applied.
Born with a gift of seeing, the artist's hands fashion a painting
    through a craft,
Springing from a soul of light.
As she gently dipped her brush into the colors of the earth,
She listened and observed.
Thus, the music of the canvas was born.
There is that moment when true inspiration comes,
When Mozart played, Einstein's brain flashed.
This painter beheld a simple act of creation, and now her light
    illumines the world
…As angels watched overhead.

Ronald Rand
St. Simons Island, GA

Of Lamar

We were boyhood friends living on adjacent farms in
northern Indiana. At thirteen, we milked cows by hand
on cold, wintry mornings and fed milk to the cats
directly from a cow's teats before going to school.
At fifteen, we swam in the Elkhart River and
the Stauffer girls came and hid our clothes.
In high school we participated in the statewide
mathematics scholarship competition.
Since neither of us enjoyed cold weather,
we chose to have our careers in Florida.
During retirement, we played bridge,
sang songs together, and reminisced about singing
"Sweetly Sings the Donkey" at a grade school
PTA meeting while his mother played the piano.
On April 19, 2015, he turned seventy-seven, and on May 13, 2015,
I visited with him the day before he left us.
As I stood by his side he clasped my hand and
projected his unique smile that embodied a grin
filled with a bit of cynicism, acknowledging the
inevitability of human existence.
He said, "I am glad to see you."

Christian M. Yoder
Athens, OH

The Russian Jeté

Weaving dancers leap across a Russian stage with flying treads
Staccato beats, sharpened turns and ringlet-piled heads

Swift turns and Eastern halts, another slipper locks the floor
Another one there raps, figurines jete forevermore

One slipper thuds upon the stage, a beat of silence sweet,
As the thousandth jete breaches the air, cream floors each toe to meet

The light does flicker in and out and eerie mumbles rise
Slippered feet still churn ballet, their holy talent prized

Grace filled dancers tumble forth, they tumble, but won't trip
The show goes on as history might, the history twixt your grip

Pitter patter grows to swell, each pinkish shoe abright
Glowing faintly in the pitch of a blackened Russian night

They catch themselves as jetés falter, but each iota grace,
They shall enter each solemn doubt, as history takes her place

The trenches of their arches, the muddiness in their turns
The withering march of every step so cold it starts to burn

The artillery of the smacking feet, the charge of heaving breath
In timeless time they keep their time—one two, three four, rest rest

Something shatters with a quake like a smite heard up above
They do not scatter, they keep their form whilst fear fits like a glove

There is nothing to be done as the pinkish glows do fade
Night pounces on the back of each to dance in war-ish shade

But the humming roars roll backwards, as night rolls off of her back
Tips of sunlight slowly kill the vulnerability of black

Wan figures, limbs, with hair unraveled
An empty hall, night newly traveled

Ava Occiahlini
Brookline, NH

Remembering

Of course elephants remember,
  I'm sure of that.
When I was a little girl,
  I was treated to a trip
To the circus with my dad.
  It was a very memorable day,
That I had.
  When we went to visit the elephants,
One greeted us by waving his trunk at me.
  When we were about to leave,
Another elephant stomped his big foot
  And told us to stay.
When we continued to depart,
  He raised up his front feet, gave a big roar,
Swinging his trunk in the air, and said,
  "You may not always remember me,
But, you will be sure I will not forget
  That you visited here, you see,
And you made a new friend."
  "You will always remember the good
Friends you have, but if you forget them,
  I would be sad.
One told you that friends are like flowers,
  And you get to pick them."
I picked one. I picked you, _____.

Florence Corrigan
Redlands, CA

Breaking Point

The voices in my head,
are as loud as a lion's roar.
The constant yelling,
drowning my thoughts.
They tell me to kill,
but the blade never stains.
They tell me to jump,
but I don't fall.
They complain about my smile,
but I don't mind.
They make jokes,
but I still laugh.
Their constant mocking,
doesn't affect me.
However,
for some reason,
my heart still aches.
"I'm fine,"
I lie,
deep inside,
my heart cries.

Joyce Chung
Oakland, CA

Angels

There are angels in the sky
that whisper words of comfort in your sleep
that wrap their soft wings around your
trembling shoulders and hold you as you cry.

They look down on you with delight
and remember you as you were when
they were there with you before they were angels
before they had to hold you at night.

And they are thankful for what you do
thankful for the angels you help keep on the ground
long before it is their time to fly to Heaven
thankful for the sad angels who turn to you.

And those sad angels are thankful too
because you are their friend, their parent,
their teacher, you are their guide to hope
to their happiness starting anew.

So your angels in Heaven whomever they may be
and the angels you help on the ground
say, "stay strong" and "thank you, angel,"
for keeping this Heaven from me.

Kristina Téa Rubertone
Manhasset, NY

A Place to Aim For

Is the sky the place to aim for
Or is there something more?
Should we aim for the stars
Or could that be just too far?

Can we reach a higher elevation,
To get closer to the constellations?
Do we climb to the highest peak,
To be able to find what we seek?

We can see the little bit of glare,
The question is, how do we get there?
The closer we get, the further it seems,
Reality starts to intertwine with dreams.

It feels like a long distance race,
We are in need of a rocket to space.
We would like to get there soon,
Even if we only get close to the moon.

We'd like to see what's out there,
To see the world beyond compare.
So, is there one place to aim for
Or is there something more?

Gregory Jean-Baptiste
Coral Springs, FL

The Call

A mighty dread had come during the night,
People cowered till the break of daylight.
Then a man woke up, knew he must harken,
To the call which has made the land darken.
This dread, which was spreading fear across the land,
Is of an impending battle, not fought in mortal hands.
It is a battle between gods, to see who is fit,
To control the people, and the land on which we sit.
So when the man heard the gods would battle,
Just to see who would be shepherd, to us cattle.
He knew he must stop this any way he could,
Even if he had to shout at the gods, as he should.
Traveling over the horizon he saw the gods,
Gathered in a circle, holding golden staffed rods.
He walked in between the gods, and shouted his words,
Telling them to be silent, so he could be heard.
The gods looked down upon this man, saw fear and love,
Love for the earth, under Heaven, in him was above.
Hearing his pleas of no battle, the gods let him speak,
Seeing in him he was strong and not weak.
Finishing and standing tall, the gods felt his mirth,
And in the next, the gods vanished from the earth.
The man looked around feeling a little lost,
Wondering why he had risked his life, a precious cost.
But then in his heart he knew,
The earth had been saved 'cause he had spoken true.

Keith Koloske
Covington, WA

Hide and Seek

When I was young
I played hide and seek with my brother
We laughed together in the fields
When my ma called we would return home
We went to war
My ma called
I came home
My brother's hidden forever
He'll never return

Tehilla Rosenberg
Dallas, TX

Crossing the Finish Line

Why does putting yourself out there get defeated by popularity?
Why does what you say have to be judged?
Why does going the extra mile lose to only one step?
Why does losing feel like heartbreak?

How can words be so timeless, yet so powerful?
How can your appearance and intelligence get overlooked?
How can people be so hurtful without knowing it?
How can words of wisdom cheer you up?

How can you win the race, if you never crossed the finish line?

Hannah Dresner
Ridgewood, NJ

The Light Outside Depression

Happiness is like a fluttering bird,
In the silence it likes to be heard
For a smile to beam from ear to ear
To wipe away all those fragile tears
For laughs to echo through the halls
Memories kept within these walls
Secrets disappear once you evolve
All of your problems will soon be solved
Hope speaks out, wishing to be heard
All bad memories soon become blurred
Your soul dances with delight
Suddenly your future seems so bright
Slowly beginning to set out and soar
Feeling so beautiful right to the core
It may not happen overnight
But before you know it, you'll be all right

Kadeelyn Nicole Konstantino
Easton, CT

Kadeelyn Konstantino is a twenty-year-old survivor of mental illness. She lives in a small town in Connecticut. Her inspiration for this poem came from going through her own personal struggles and then rising above. Her mission is to give hope to others and encourage them to fight their battles, because she knows if they try and give it their all, that they too can overcome anything.

Penguins

Penguins slip and slide
They show off all of their pride
They waddle around

Gentoos, emperors,
Rockhoppers, and little blues,
Happiness is bound

Sliding across ice,
Sweet, caring, and oh so nice,
Love is always found

Kate E. Pipes
Colleyville, TX

Betrayal

Lost in dreams of endless wonder
I now wake from a long slumber
Seeing colors in black and white
Crossing the barriers of space and light
I am brought back to life
Only to feel the sharp knife
Stealing my chi once again
Saying goodbye to your dearest friend
Only wanting your own pain to end

Brianna Elder-Clark
Jonesboro, AR

Faith

Unseen
It is there
For us to feel
To keep us pushing to the horizon

Pulling those that hide behind the dark moon
To test our strength
His purpose
Brings us
He

Keeps
Our dreams
Hears our hearts
The universe
It's the ministry that heals his people

We
Our... art
We breathe life
The world... our stage
What we do is give it to humankind...

Jody-lynne Nicole Austin
Pennsauken, NJ

Jody Austin is a professional registered nurse and retired veteran of the United States Air Force. She has been writing since she was a child and enjoys sharing her poetry with others. She is also cofounder of the Collective Mic arts organization in the Philadelphia, PA, area.

Intima

Lover of the falling stars and whispering screams,
the columbine petals buried beneath leaves.
Able to gaze and smile at the marigold beams,
the blades of pity her strongest foe.
Feeling this game of chance has turned to chess,
the tight-lipped smile of the stranger so dear.
She wonders of the genie's lamp,
those tales of triumph that afire her year.
Yet she fears the self-built cage of glass,
the rose tinted panes reflect her mind.
Wishing flight along with the birds of paradise,
the billions of fireflies blazing one final time.
Dreaming of the world so fresh, so young, so bold,
her place in the garden of life untold.

Nicole Victoria Rychagov
Virginia Beach, VA

Comatose

I am hungry
But I do not wish to be fed.
My feet are beginning to blister
But I allow myself to be led.
My opinion is great
But I will not voice in debate.
Others can often criticize
I am afraid of the repetitive hate.
The days flash forward
But I will not open my eyes.
As life cycles I never stop to realize
Who am I?

With change comes sacrifice
And with me I do not take advice.
I walk down the street with my head down
But you will never see me with a frown.
I wear a mask, hidden by my fears
And by this my death feels ever so near.

Jill Marie Sullivan
Angola, NY

The Game of Colors

You had told me it's okay, that you care
I told you I believed you even though you couldn't bare
Your words led me not, your opinion in two
Your respect in disguise, the lying only grew
You swore it was okay, as you had mentioned before
You had said I was loved even though my heart was very sore
I knew you didn't believe, how didn't I know
You had deceived and the lying will only grow
You pulled me into your little tricks
The game of colors destroyed my defensive bricks
You had decided that you were red, I was forced to be blue
Though through all the chaos it seemed as if purple wasn't for you
I had loved you, I didn't know why but it was true
I wish I hadn't, but you were you
More than you know, deeper than you think
During every second, heartbeat, blink
I wish you had opened your eyes and seen the truth
You should've understood me from the root
I had told you not to be confused, to please understand
Oh, I became broken just saying I loved you in the end

Claire Shamiya
Henderson, NV

As an upcoming freshman, I realized that I wanted to make a contribution to the world through poetry. Books, movies, songs and even not-so-talked-about challenges are the inspiration for my writing. Realism is what I strive towards. Also poetry is one way I express myself. Furthermore, without the love and support from my family it wouldn't be possible.

The Gull

Where are the ashes that you stole
Their sanctity not yet complete.
The priest had just begun
The holy words, the ancient rite to mark his duty done.
Do olden ways reside in you that we no longer know?
Are you a scavenger of souls come to gather
The brightest and the best?
We watched 'til we no longer saw your graceful form
Tracking the river's lazy roll.
Careless you flew, your wings outstretched
So like a priestly form at Eucharist.
At length we turned once more to earthly duties.
There was no need to stay.
The object of our prayers was gone.
Your deft wings had taken ashes, grief and prayers
And we were freed.

Ella Chapman Dunn
Lompoc, CA

Humanity

Hath the time passed so slowly
Under the sun, clouds or rain
Man growing day by day
All of nature surrounding
Nature or nurture, what could be the difference?
I, a part of the human race, declare
Thous't own home
Your decree of destruction

Aamnah Mansoor Allawala
Austin, TX

Poetry of the Dead

The living poetry that is your movement
fades as the last dead leaf touches cold ground.
Watch closely; the last breath comes once.
And then, within a sobering fraction of a moment,
death's secret is revealed.
A sensation of breaking water after being submerged,
lungs gasping for air, and finding it —
in dying this liberation is continuous,
until, at individual pace, the air transforms
into a kind of salvation and all sense of
struggle is devoured by overwhelming waves.

Patrick Louis Rieser
Clarksburg, WV

Circles

Why do we always run in circles?
We run and we run until our paths cross again
Then we try and run in the opposite direction
But you're a force of nature and
I always come back in your direction

When we start to run again that's when the rain falls down
And we're miserable and gloomy like the clouds
But when our paths cross again time stands still and
We stand there staring at each other
Wondering which one of us is going to run first this time
But when we collide it's
Like fireworks shooting off in the heavenly sky
But then you get scared again and take off running
And I take off chasing after you
When we try and part our separate ways
There's this magnetic force that pulls us back

I'm pretty sure if I ripped my heart out in front of you
And told you to keep it
You'd take off running with it and not give me yours
Every once in a while you'd come back with it and put it back
Where it belongs
Then you'd take off again
And now we're back to running in circles

Elizabeth Michelle Adzema
San Dimas, CA

Moving On

You were with us for a while and now you take flight
on golden wings made of everlasting light

When the sun shines we will think of your smile
laughing and dancing in God's beautiful Nile

On to a land much better than this
to find your peace, to find your bliss

You now move forward to join the angels glorious meet
beyond the gate, beyond the street

Some will smile and fake it through
some will cry and mourn the death of you

Each will move on and find our way
because we know we will see you again someday

Clare Brown
Anaconda, MT

Distance of Love

When I was to ask a question of her
Something I was pondering about more and more

What is the farthest distance between you and your love?
Is it the absence of feelings and nothing but fluff?

Is it the choices and rejections you make?
Or is it something you look for, like fate?

Something I though of myself and said forth:
It's that your love does not know you exist on this earth!

"No dear…," she answered in tears of passion and fire
(It's the feeling of standing right near the one you desire),
"The feeling of being so close, and yet galactically far
Afraid to feel my heart tear and scar"

(Here you are, but frozen I stay
Not knowing what can I possibly say
Keeping my silence — I live in decay
Just praying for that one special day)

Mikhail Nepomnyashchiy
Brooklyn, NY

Trapped

No more tears; we will cry until the day —
a day that will never come, because it has already passed.
Just dried tears cake my face, but I still cry.
I must have dried the ducts that fills my eyes,
'cause nothing comes like nothingness, empty just like me.

Corey Dean George
Avon, OH

I Can't Explain It Mom

I can't explain it Mom,
the way he makes me feel.
Those butterflies in my stomach I felt on our first date,
have expanded throughout my whole body.
With every touch he ignites my skin like a fire.
Every laugh he laughs I fall deeper in love with him.
He makes me feel extraordinary, like I'm more than just a girl.
He makes this more than a teenage love, he makes it true.
He makes me feel _____.
I could insert a million words there,
it wouldn't do this love justice.
You felt this once right?
I can't explain it Mom.

Mariah Hammond
Orleans, IN

The Temptress of the Solstice

Sweet summer breezes tame the heart on fire
How slowly the world turned for you, turned for me

Light green eyes swim in a sea of wonder
They electrocute the skin of a new explorer

Drifting and fading from euphoria to a parallel universe
One that allows gentle words to make a temptress
   completely entranced

The inconceivable charm
That leaves the lips of a clone is so new to be bestowed upon

Perhaps when awoken from this dream
The smoke from the flame will still be burning within my head

Dayna Sammartino
North Lima, OH

The Court Room

Sunlight illuminates
a solemn room.
Dust particles float aimlessly
much like my thoughts.

I sit motionless,
a cold and barren bench,
praying for mercy,
for him, for me.

Distinct sounds of clinking chains,
chorus of lost souls,
Moving in unison,
Brightly clad in orange and black.

My beautiful child,
staring hopelessly —
a captured soul,
his innocence held hostage.

I glance at the clock,
stuck on past dreams.
Locked into self torment,
a dark sadness overcomes me.

Pat Nichols
Edmond, OK

My poems come from my twenty-year journey through addiction with my child, a journey that took us to dark places we never dreamed possible. It is also a journey of love, hope, compassion and recovery — a life journey that changed everyone in the family, a change that has given us a new purpose, one with peace and serenity.

Wake Up

People only listen when I stop talking
Will only appreciate me when I stop walking.

Can't make time to help a stranger
That to me, is the real danger.

But how could we as a people move forward?
By working together, like we all should.

We have more tools now than ever.
Now we have fools that don't work together.

People value race over life.
Fighting with words has been replaced with a knife.

War is not the answer, for sure,
But this has all happened before.

People need to take up a stand.
We don't need to break up the band.

Hopefully, the masses get quite a shake up,
Maybe big enough, for all of you to wake up.

Paul Ethan Bagley
Durand, IL

Ode to the Dew

Spring mornings filled with new life
My feet in the wet fresh cut grass
My brother holds my hand with a gentle grasp
We play with worms coming from the ground
My pink dress becoming tarnished
My smile becoming wider my feet dirtier
I look at my mother coffee in her hand
My father's newspaper covering him from view
My grandfather sleeping in the lawn chair
My grandmother smiling widely at us kids playing
My happiness known by a sweet giggle
My love for life known by the kind embrace of my brother
Now I'm older and no longer a child
I again sit in the morning dew
With a small stream of tears dripping down my face
My brother in the corner looking out to the distance
My mother with a tissue in her hand
My father with his hands covering him from view
My grandfather's head down as if sleeping
My grandmother no longer smiling no longer awake
Sadness glued onto my face shown with a sob
My hate for life known by the cold glare of my brother
I sit next to the stone carved with my beloved grandmother's name
I'm not quite alive but not quite dead
That child playing in the dew and fresh cut grass is far from here
For I am gone with the wind not coming back

Anna Lalumondier
Shawnee, KS

Heartfelt Dreams

My heartfelt dreams
  keep bursting like bubbles
After each wafts
  lovely, full, iridescent and round
Disheartening it is
  most certainly
To witness each dream
  implode and feebly vanish
Into the depth of some convenient,
  nonchalant nearby ground

Jennifer Tahtinen
Webster, WI

Jennifer Tahtinen has been writing since childhood. Misguided and mistaken, she later perceived herself to be a promising screenwriter while penning pages of poetry. Living in rural serenity, Jennifer writes almost daily despite being never the same upon the demise of Lucera Linda ("lovely bright star"), her beloved Peruvian horse. "Heartfelt Dreams" is pulled from Jennifer's "Roadside Beauty" stack.

Frail Flaw

Towards the end of a brilliant day quite near the shore,
The golden sun beams as it sets, for prime is the hour.
There in the warm washed sands of time are faded footprints where
Once stood a woman, in whose youth-filled hair laid a vibrant flower.
'Twas not her alone that stood in the sand; next to her shadow,
A man stood tall, firm, and grounded: his radiance full of power.

Into their souls they each did gaze with
Passion, affection, and yearning!
Marriage was seized, thus united
They were in a love that was burning!

Oh dying sun, beyond the waves, that pricks the horizon,
Thy beams reveal saddening truth: that their love cannot last.
The memory, though grand it may be of a wedding feat,
Has but one frail flaw, the time embraced towards now is passed.
Love is real and must endure, though kings rule not this thing!
All oaths not bound nor sealed, into the ocean they are cast!

Oh Passion and Mystery, and
Far spent yearning, with all love brings,
Grasp the burning, blazing, pure, boundless
Meaning within those binding rings!

Shawn Howe
Elko, NV

Life Is a Roller Coaster

Life is a roller coaster
It has ups and downs
Loops and sharp turns
Sometimes, you just want to scream
And other times,
You just want to enjoy the ride
There are periods of excitement
Times when your stomach drops

But at the end of the ride,
You are able to look back
And find meaning
And you just want to do it again and again
Because it would not be the same
Without the screams and excitement
Life has meaning
But we may have to wait until the end
To be able to see it

Alexa Cohen
Hollywood, FL

Misunderstood

I don't know her everyday I cross paths with a beautiful woman
Beautiful in the way that she brings beauty into the world
Humble, a pastel on the canvas of New York
Eyes down cast lips upturned hair flowing
It hums live simply love deeply and laugh often
I call her the mystery woman hiding behind the mask
Because after all this time I've yet to see her eyes
Admiration is farthest from understanding

Tomorrow will be different
Her baby blue denim shirt rolled up at the sleeves
Unbuttoned not too much, tails untucked, I will…
Cast a glance in her direction an overcast of sunlight obliterating
Her face
But as the clouds of sunlight clear
I will be surprised to see
Two grey eyes looking back at me…

Ramadhan Ahmad
New York, NY

A Girl's Best Friend

Do you and your best friend have a close bond?
Perhaps you share a special song?

Your best friend may be lazy,
But you can always turn her into crazy.

Does she ever sneak your blouse?
Like a tiny little mouse?

Do you ever lose your pants?
Then find out she's wearing them at dance?

Your best friend should always be loyal.
And never let your secrets get spoiled.

Have you ever gone to a campfire together?
Perhaps in chilly weather.

Your best friend should be caring.
And always very sharing.

If you are a best friend back,
Your friendship will stay on track.

Samantha Lynn Kelly
Clear Lake, WI

On Butterfield Lake

Awakened gently by the song of the locals
that serenade each wave,
we contentedly hesitate to stir
from our relaxed state.

The scent of the coming feast,
prepared by our generous hostess,
comes from the kitchen
and meanders its way
to our sleeping quarters.

Swaggering, we sleepily anticipate
the smorgasbord placed before us
as if breakfast fulfilled
desired prophecies.

The tender sprinkling
of the sun in the morning
baptizes the day in warmth
by noon when our agendas commence.

Afternoon fades into dusk
and we return to the chalet
where forms of lore, literature and film
entertain until sirens of slumber call to us
once more.

Seth Burky
Canton, OH

Exposed

Your arms may be open now,
soaking up the energy of the crowd
just like the rays of the sun

It feels good, great in fact
I understand, it's like soaring through the clouds

But soon sweetheart that sun,
it'll turn to rain
and your white shirt will be see-through

Once you're exposed there is no going back
what's done is done
it's as if you're a goner
and really it's because you are

So I hope you'll listen before
you put your thoughts on paper
or even in words

Think twice before you're so sure
that what's exposed can be hidden

Grace Ryanne Carico
Meridian, ID

This Is What I Want

I want to wake up in your bed
with your plaid shirt buttoned over
my naked body,
and my hair rustled from the pillows
cushioning my mind
and my head resting on your warm bare chest
and my fingers entwined with yours.
I want your lips pressed
against my forehead
and your body hovering close to mine
so that our breaths mingle
and we are
one.
I want you on a Sunday morning
when the sun is just peeking through
the dark window
and the coffee is bubbling
wildly upstairs.
I want sunny side up eggs
and toast stained with burns and
doused with butter.
I want your hand on the small of my back
peering over a pan
of sizzling salty bacon.
I want to grow wrinkly and gray
with you in that moment
forever.

Nicolette Petnuch
Yonkers, NY

Grandpa's Hands

Grandpa's hands are strong and steady.
They are simple yet so complex.
They do not scold or correct.
They hold me when I cry.
They carry me when I am tired.
They teach me how to work.

Grandpa's hands are now weak.
They show the stories of age.
They no longer work long days.
They now hold the hands of the ones he loves.
They teach me how to love.
They grow weaker each day.

Grandpa's hands are folded at peace.
They, for the first time, are still.
They now hold a memory in my heart.
They remind me of the good times and bad.
One day his hands will be in mine again.

Hailey Ewy
Westbrook, MN

Grotesque Lullaby

Approached by a bleak and dismal entity,
Who murmurs a cascade of elegant tunes,
A serene somnolent lullaby,
Uttered with the guarantee of unending euphoria,
Thus beguiled in the assurance of an indefinite elixir,
Stricken into a state of everlasting delirium,
An eternal hysteria,
Grasping for evanescent reality in vain.
The wisps of that lullaby materialize around you,
Such a sedative melody,
Arising within you not the deception of rationality,
But the actuality of forfeited sanity.
The dreary entity departs,
Shadowed by the unhinging wisps of the song,
Conceived to craze, dement, and derange,
Call it a grotesque lullaby.

Erin Elizabeth Chappell
Havana, AR

Parting

His wrinkled face barely able to muster a smile
His wife was away, she had been gone for a while
His back ached and his hands were cold
Only a few days more, he had been told

He was once afraid of the day,
The day, the last day, he would be on the earth to stay
Yet he was not afraid, he felt enlightened
A full life he had lived, no reason to be frightened

His vision was blurred, but he could see the light
He had no more feeling, but he felt right
His eyes closed, breathing his last shallow breaths
This is not the end... this is only death

Ben Floren
Cotuit, MA

No Laments

A destroyed world, a nonsense idea.
Things that I no longer know... no laments.

The father who no longer exists... blessed, blissful, welcomed.
The mother faded into oblivion... nothingness.
Things that change, that's it... no laments.

My crying heart... no laments.
My mind is racing... in hurry... alive... no laments.
Everything changes, everything goes by... no laments.

Children without parents.
Parents without parents.
Souls fluctuating in the blank space...
Eternal and masters of themselves.

An embittered deep sigh... down on the ground.
Poor little angel, let him sleep, just... justified by God.
He didn't turn seven yet, he can't be sinful... paralysis.

Courtesy of selfish parents...
Paranoid, psychotic, rotten paraphernalia, but for who?
For those who pay the debt of lunatics and their ruined ancestors.

She still waits... she is tired of looking for the others...
She is tired of dying each day.
She, a fairy, deceptive, compulsory.
Oh! It's done!

Adriana Kaye
Millerton, NY

Adriana Kaye is an educator who graduated with honors in Spanish language and literature. She is passionate about English and Latin American literature, writing, photography and travelling with her husband. Her inspiration to write comes from her life experiences and her culturally diverse background. Besides poetry, Adriana Kaye is the author of numerous academic articles on education and literary analysis.

Townsfolk

The young women are flowering. Their fathers:
skinny balsa and winter is just around the bend.
All newborns are sun-drops to wedded mothers: what
can be said of the dying widow — her body a desert

barren. Her blonde lover framed on the kitchen countertop.
Who will sing her rotting form to sleep?
Somewhere on the coast a light
guides a fisherman home. Nets alive,

seething with snow-bellied fish. Hands pruned and
salted. His children will grow and want
for nothing. Sub-zero winds ascend teen bodies knot

behind closed doors. Think of the people as
sand clinging to the shoreline. An ebb and flow of fleshy
ultramarine. They are the crumbs of light in the morn:

the glossy stardust
in our eye teeth.

Jason Guisao
Floral Park, NY

Man of Integrity

Many years of loving you have made me realize,
An image you have given me coming from a daughter's eyes.
No one will ever know what's true unless spoken from the heart.
Only I can say these words, so from my lips they'll part.
For you alone deserve so much, as anyone can see.
It's on my mind and in my soul that you will always be.
Never losing sight of this and trying to be strong.
Take courage and the deepest strength, which you've had all along.
Everyone must grin and bear the trials of their day.
God gave you the gift of love to make it through that way.
Reading anything I write may bring someone to tears.
It's seeing you for who you are, that's brought me up these years.
Today I am reminded of something I've come to see.
You've been my rock and dearest friend, man of integrity.

Hope Taubinger
Cicero, NY

Kingdom Come

I dreamt I was king of the world
The world was on the head of a pin
I took the pin and shoved it into my eye
It was only then that I could see my kingdom,
Clearly

Kenneth Lee Menear
Virginia Beach, VA

The Dragon

Can't you one day just grab me
look me in the eyes and say, I know you're not okay
now stop acting like you are
and when I scream from the pain
that the dragon has put me through for so long
you just hold me through it all
and you will hold me when the dragon
tells me I am worthless and pathetic
for you know your love is all I need but
life has never been a fairy tale and you are no prince
but my pain is the dragon in all of the
fairy tales and he sure looks a lot like you

Sydney Goldeman
East Bethel, MN

Earthworm Flies

The rain came down
saturating the ground
The earthworm came up
to swim in the muck

The dove came down
hearing a splish-splash sound
Now the earthworm flies

James Hyler II
Monroe, VA

Two Stars Two Sunsets

Come join the conga line in the constellations
Tango among the twinkling stars
Move over Lucy
There are also planets in the sky with diamonds
One third of planet Cancri e is pure diamond
Planets it seems are a girl's best friend
Clouds in space have the chemical that makes up raspberries and rum
Anyone up for some drunken giant berry picking
Tugging at the threads of nature we find the truth
Like 500 fiendish kittens left in a room with 500 balls of yarn
And the sweater of the universe was mad

Dave Shorr
Buffalo Grove, IL

Let Us Gather Elder Blossom

Let us gather elder blossom,
Sing the song of circumstance,
Let the awful with the awesome
Go and dance their spiral dance;

As the chiral shadows shuffle,
Saturated with azure,
Laughing with unlawful muffle
Footsteps darkness reassure.

Universe of chances, choices—
None can ever understand—
Time inverts; invested voices
Echo empty in the hand.

Let the steps unearth the nether
Dwellers and their occult schemes,
Draw through coiling smoke a feather—
Let us swirl-up further dreams.

Mark Meyerzon
Northbrook, IL

Cries

The cries heard from the
Crowd of the youth burn
With the death of the thought
That once upon a time will always
End in a happily ever after, only
To be found at the bottom of the
Valley of darkness, covered in
Black tar, sucking them into the
Never ending truth that love is
Not always forever.

Brenden Mariage
Holt, MI

Memorial Day

In the air, on land and sea,
they volunteered so willingly,
and fought against our enemies,
for you and I to live life free.
Laid down their lives so selflessly,
remember them immortally,
with honor, courage and bravery.
They're loved and missed so desperately,
forever may they rest in peace.

Adam Dague
Kent, WA

The Glory of Spring

The snow melts away,
Revealing lush, green grass,
Making a soft playground for critters to play.

White and yellow daffodils bud and then bloom;
They dot the landscape with colors of cheer,
They take away Winter's white and gray gloom.

Fuzzy caterpillars burst forth into thousands of butterflies;
They delight in their wings and display their outfits of color;
It's a beautiful sight as they and Spring harmonize.

Streams that once were solid ice begin to freely flow,
To endow life to each blade of grass, tree and flower;
Every river, lake, and burbling brook puts on quite a show.

Every living thing is renewed and becomes revived;
It was like Winter never came and laid her white earth,
When Spring and the life she brings have finally arrived.

Teresa Victoria Hill
Copperhill, TN

A Whole in One

A hole in one,
There's room for two,
A need in me, a space for you.
This could be fun,
I jest, I pun
To hide the blue
As you pass through
Like rays of the sun.

You too, and I,
That makes three,
All for my
Own trinity.
We merge, I die,
One whole in we.

Stephen John Groak
La Mirada, CA

I am originally from the South, the Deep South — New Zealand, growing up in West Auckland. I currently live in Los Angeles County with my wife, four daughters and a menagerie of other critters. The poem, "A Whole in One," is inspired by Paramahansa Yogananda.

Abraham Lincoln

Abraham Lincoln was a towering figure among men,
With his black stovepipe hat he stood six foot ten,
His intellect soared higher than that,
He could outwit and win in a fight or a spat,
As a lawyer he won the most difficult cases,
And always found evidence in small unseen traces
He rose to great heights of power,
He could say in a few words what others wrote in pages
At Gettysburg he became one among sages,
No other president had such moral standing
With a stroke of a pen slavery was disbanding,
A nation he saved from being a house divided,
Reconciliation of North and South he had decided
It all ended tragically one night,
When an assassin caused massive fright
A shot was fired to end the great emancipator,
At a showing of *An American Cousin* in Ford's Theater,
Great men seem to have a tragic ending,
Because they have uncommon courage without bending
Cowards will always strike down achievers,
Because they are fundamental deceivers,
Who want to make a mark in a history book
In the end their lives meaning they forsook,
Because a man's sacred honor they took

Ronald Taylor Stotts
Brookfield, CT

I am a poet of everyday people. My poems include famous people, history, science, culture, religion, humor and nature. This poem was inspired by visiting many sites associated with Abraham Lincoln and reading many volumes about his life. He stands out among presidents for his integrity, honor and courage. My wife and I are retired and live in Brookfield, Connecticut. I am a graduate of Indiana University in Bloomington, Indiana.

Blue Bird

Little Blue Bird up high in the sky
Can you tell her for me that I loved her
From the start
And that this comes from my very heart
Oh little Blue Bird high in the sky

Little Blue Bird up high in the sky
Please find her for me oh at least
Tell me why
Oh I miss her tonight oh I loved her
From the start
And this comes from the heart
Little Blue Bird up high in the sky

Yes tell her for me that I loved her
Right from the very start.
Oh Little Blue Bird in the sky
Oh little Blue Bird in the — sky.

Marshall Neal Dayjr
Garland, TX

Did You

Did you see they bled red when you shot them dead
It's the same blood red you would shed
It's not okay any day
In any way
Black or white
Stop the fight
We all have joy
We all have pain
We are all different
And we are all the same
Hurting, hating and killing each other
It's the most horrible shame
Did you see your young one in his early state
He would play with any and all
Without a care at all
Why oh why would you fill him with hate

Erin Diffenderfer
Anderson, SC

Nursery Rhymes Filled with Love

Scientists claim you can hear even before you're born
That someone can talk to a cotton-covered beating heart
And your ears will memorize the sounds
Before you know what a sound is
They also claim that this builds a level of love
Trust
Bonding on a deeper level
But what I've been trying to explain to them
Is that soul mates must be found whispering in the nursery
After everyone has left
Because the only explanation for hearing a voice
And finally feeling at home
Is that their voice
Is what took you home in the first place
The smile filled windowpanes in a hospital room
Thousands of miles away
Were built with the voice of someone still crying out for you
Sixteen years later
When you are unable to love them back
And although the screams
Will never be enough to fill the memories of someone else
Please remember to cherish the way you trust them
And love them
And have bonded with them
In the least scientifically explainable way possible

Carlee Ann Lightle
Mount Vernon, OH

Rise

Moon glows on black waters —

Closed eyes
arms spread —
wings of sand bound to my back
sea waves drag me in,
not letting go.
I can't go on. Anymore.
The howl
calling for victory
invisible claw prints march across my mind.

My eyes open —
Coyote's yellow eyes stare at me.
Hot breath, my breath, our breath
I rise.
Sand wings fall,
Raven wings grow,
I fly.

Cristina Cortez
Williston Park, NY

I'm a first-generation Latin-American poet born to immigrant parents. I happen to have cerebral palsy, and I'm bound to a wheelchair. I dedicate myself to the art of writing fiction, poetry, and travel writing. I'm fortunate to travel all over the world and aspire to launch my blog, www.travelonwheels.org. Its purpose will be to raise awareness about accessibility while exploring disability etiquette. My preferred genres are historical fiction, fantasy and free-verse. The poem "Rise" was written to describe a dream, but like any true piece of art, it's open to readers' interpretations.

A Lurking Friend

A girl that no one cared for,
Treading a dark path with no stop.
She was being followed by a dark figure,
Thought to be a monster.
She could hear it dragging its legs,
She could feel his eyes piercing through her.
The girl began to speed up her pace,
But so did the fellow creeping behind her.
The faster she ran forward,
The more swiftly he'd move.
There was a delay in her swiftness,
A branch which she had stumbled on.
She shrieked in deep dismay,
Only to find out,
The monster was there to help.

Dixie Rose Kearsch
Davie, FL

Paranoia

It seeps through your skin
walking on your brain
terrorizing your mind
driving you insane
It creeps up on you
like a shadow with no shape
it clutches your lungs hard
allowing no air to escape
You run so fast
but the shadow follows as your own
you try to hide away
but it's only grown
You shake, you tremble
but there's no change
it haunts your soul
and you feel strange
It touches your skin
and penetrates through
you try to run again
but it's inside of you
You just stand and stare
with nothing to hear
everything to see
and everything to fear

Rhonda Graham
Orange Beach, AL

Freedom

The air is cold
As the look on my master's face
I hear the wind speak my name

A lot depends on me getting free
Distant echoes of angry voices fill the air
They're coming for me

I need to hurry
Run as fast as my legs will take me
Coming to a stop

As I feel the trees for moss
It points to the north
My freedom

I look to the moon for courage
Clutching my chest as I try to catch my breath
Running faster and faster

To my freedom

Abby D. Evans
Gahanna, OH

The Moonlight

I remember the day that I was afraid
The day that Hope ran away
In her arms was my heart
That she had taken from the very start
There was a fire in my heart that day
The day she looked my way
She blew me a kiss
That I made sure not to miss
The love was sweet but not meant to last
But that is all in the past
My heart is gone now that she stole it away
And now it's time that I must sway
From the branch that's high in the air
As I drop I will have no care
1, 2, 3
Then that's it for me
But as I'm about to drop
A voice calls out that tells me to stop
Hope appears and in her arms is my heart, but something's new
My one heart is now made of two
This must mean our love is not done
So this means there is no need to run
And as the moon comes out to play
I realize that Hope is here to stay

Lian Thomas Parent
Hampden, ME

Who Are You Inside

Everyone thinks different, just like me
Everyone sees the same, just like me
Everyone is afraid to exist, just like me
Everyone is afraid of themselves, just like me

Everyone hides their true self because they don't know
If they will be accepted
I've learned one thing, would you tell the younger you to hide
If you met a young child and they had the same insecurities as you
What would you tell him or her?

Would you tell them they're not perfect?
Would you tell them they're a mistake?
Would you tell them they weren't beautiful to be called magnificent?
Would you hurt them, bruise them, shame them
What would you say to them, if they ask you for help?
If they ask you what you thought of them

You know what I would say
I would say you're perfect and spiritually perfect
I would say you are strong and will grow up to be someone's hero
I would say you're beautiful and don't let anyone tell you otherwise
What would you say?

Yehuwdiyth Y. Yodhhewawhe
Celebration, FL

Pop Goes the Ego

She is the mistress of sexual spectacle.
She only wants to perform a respectable
Part in the pantheon of the perfectible
Idols of glamour and show.
Molting her vestments, she enters the manic scene
Chanting her mantras from dramas and magazines,
Dancing with cameras and light in a frantic dream,
Chasing down fame's flitting glow.
Buoyed by worship, she reaches her pinnacle,
Making her prey to the hostile and cynical.
Parasite acolytes seal her within a cool
Chrysalis, capturing her form.
Now her friends gaze on her, never to talk or stay.
Lovers turned liars by avarice walk away
Leaving her: only a little girl locked away
Far from all softness and warmth.
High on her mount she looks ever more fearfully
Out from behind a façade crafted carefully,
Hiding all sutures lest they start to tear, fully
Severing prosthetic appeal.
Knowing she's mortal, she clutches her offerings,
Using diversions and opiates to mend her seams,
Salving her doom with a mordant of self-extreme,
Never again to be real.

Adam Berk
Beverly, MA

Adam grew up in San Diego, California, before moving to Los Angeles to study film and become a struggling actor/writer. After ten years of that nonsense, he realized that playing make-believe was a silly way to make a living and the business surrounding it, even sillier. He now lives in Salem, Massachusetts, where he's found much more worthwhile means of subsistence: making up stories and mixing libations while wheedling tips from alcoholics.

A Brave Soul

Hush now, don't be scared,
On the darkest of nights,
In the dimmest of lights,
I will be there, to guide you through,
A brave soul,
Right next to you.
This brave soul, is part of you,
Through thick and thin,
I will be there.
So hush now, don't be scared.

Emily Rose Bryant
Staten Island, NY

My name is Emily Rose Bryant, and I am twelve years old. I live with my mother, two older brothers and my grandmother. We live on Staten Island in NY. Other than writing poems, I love drawing, anime, hanging out with friends, talking, and playing horror games. I wrote this poem when I was just eleven years old. This poem was inspired by two characters, Mike and Faith, from one of my games; their stories are very confusing, however Faith would always be there protecting Mike, always there for him through thick and thin, even at near death experiences.

tick, tock

tick, tock, tick, tock, tick, tock:
as the seconds go by on the clock,
life goes by one second at a time.
what will you do with your time?
tick, tock, the seconds go by on the clock.

you may waste your time,
you may live your time,
but your time is yours and yours alone,
so don't spend it alone,
or else you will waste your time.

life is too good to pass by,
so please don't cry.
don't waste any seconds.
no need to count the seconds.
don't let life pass by.

make every minute count.
make life count:
not just your life,
but every life.
make every life you know count.

Creighton Lafever
Williston, FL

My Generation

As a nineties child, I can't believe the things that I have seen.
We were in a new millennium before I was a teen.

As I was growing up, I watched as cell phones shrank and shrank;
I watched as, more and more, my parents grew to fear the bank.

When I was eight, the Twin Towers fell, which shook us to our core;
Everyone was scared, but I wasn't sure what for.

I witnessed the election of our first black president;
some thought him the devil, others thought him heaven-sent.

VCRs became obsolete right before my eyes!
And I watched as folks in Denver made sure pot was legalized!

I've seen a lot in the two decades that I've been on this earth.
The past was gone before I realized what it all was worth.

The future's here, the future's now, who knows what it will bring?
I hope my kids, in forty years, are wondering the same thing.

Hanna Marie Jones
Point Pleasant, OH

The Temperature of Burning Books

I want to read
and I want to write.
But just that isn't enough.
I want to find the words that changed people.
Where is *Uncle Tom's Cabin* and *1984?*
I want the words that offended
And began civil wars
And led the people to riot
And the government to make glorious sacrifices
To the stars and moon
Of these dead trees with black ink
Spilled all over
That turned red when the flames got past the cover
To the meat inside.
I want to find the words that burned the world,
The words that changed society,
The words that were wildfire,
Spreading,
Racing,
Coursing,
Burning everything they touch
And leaving a whiff of smoke
Because change can only happen
On a molecular level
And I have always wanted
To write fire.

Laura Duffield
Springfield, OR

Strangers Asleep on a Bus

Sand in the hourglass is slipping
In the beginning I couldn't guess which feet were mine
As the wind ran unseen fingers across my face
Under the shadow of a minor mountain.

The faint accent marks of farewell
Are prismatic bridal trains draped as veils of mist
Stars blink their hesitant hyphens
While clouds weave apostrophes over the moon.

Our landscape offers no panorama
Except views from drained cisterns
Limbs of leviathans as sycamores
Stretch to 30 degrees of sky.

Wood carvings crushed by wheelbarrows, sputters from his lips
As he mumbles of catfish and rice wine
Crossing cornfields while discreetly stepping through daffodils
In rustling weeds, choking on golden coins, a choice.

He removes his hand from mine,
And I feel naked without it;
My re-imagined past skated inside my eye lip
Whispers of dancing in the dawn; refracting pink morning
He does not know he has completed my sentence; neither do I.

Mitra Roychowdhury
New York, NY

An Invocation to Muse Beethoven

Sing to me the song, Muse Beethoven, the elixir of sorrow and spirit
written with wisdom and sentiment from tools of crafted intellect,
composed on the wrinkled papers of time.
Many relish in the passion developed within your essence,
many journeys people undertake, experienced within depths
  of minds,
the tune of life encompassed in that final note.
But I fear not see the true simplicity of the song, hard as I strive —
the obscureness of my complicated ways
leaves me in a weird world needing meaning, the song of hues
  and hope
and the melody, nostalgic, providing different emotions to the soul.
Show me the way, Muse, ode to music,
Start from where you please, and I, ready and seeking understanding,
will follow.

Nicole Teichner
Glen Allen, VA

One Day a Day Will Come

One day a day will come when you will slowly rise
That day you'll learn to live, just put your fears aside
That day you'll find a reason and the path from where you came
That day you'll carry all those dreams and give them all a name
That day you'll stand in front of everything you fear to face
That day you'll fly after all those goals you wish to chase
That day you'll win the toughest of all those bloody wars
That day you'll look back up again and wish upon those stars
That day you'll carry hope and capture all the sun's light
That day you'll get back on your feet and once again you'll fight
That day you'll wipe your tears but your ambition will be strong
That day you'll fight alone, but you'll take your strength along
That day you'll slowly burn and every inch of you will fall apart
That day you'll gather all those pieces and say you've had enough
That day you'll slay failure and you'll fight without your sword
That day you'll seize determination and victory will be yours
That day you'll walk on the fire and every piece of glass
That day you'll smile to yourself and say you're here at last
That day you'll win, as soon as you spark up the courage to try
That day will be today, the day when you slowly rise

Aisha Munir
Long Island City, NY

A Knight

You say you will never hurt me,
Nor will you ever lie,
But I am not your average girl;
You're just like every guy.

You say that I am beautiful,
Brighter than the sun.
You say that you're in love;
I am your only one.

My knight and shining armor:
A myth, fairy tale, and lie,
You say what I want to hear,
Like every other guy.

Love at first sight:
A fallen angel from the sky,
The three words you say,
Like every other guy.

No one is perfect like the
Image of a knight,
No need to be my fairy tale;
Just be my only light.

Teresa Xochitl Villanueva Proa
Sacramento, CA

Ode to a Cyclone Fence

Pigeons are perched atop your silver prongs
Preparing to fly or gaze or sleep.
Those tiny daggers used to prick our palms —
We thought we could scale you unscathed.
The boys got a running start and hit your silver sheet at full force.
Sounding like airborne loose change,
You shimmered in the sunlight.
You glowed in the lamplight.
Stretching and yawning, the posts held you while you held us.
Ascending climbers escaped the enemy:
A dog, someone's mom, a dad's whistles.
PF Flyers, small-sized and common,
Fit perfectly into each diamond link.
Petit hands grasped the sterling wires — climbing higher and higher
Up and over
Into an unsuspecting yard.

Donna Marie Abbate
Los Angeles, CA

Addicted

Leave me,
Please,
But stay.
I am alone here,
With my thoughts and my bad habits,
While my thoughts are all about you,
I dare to fathom,
Were you a bad habit of mine?
An addiction I couldn't let go of,
For fear of losing my high?
Darling,
Come back.
Let me drink in your words,
Falsely letting go of the pain.
My mind hates you,
While my heart cannot follow,
The example my mind has set.
Baby,
I need you.
It is past wanting you,
It is more than a crave.
You are my bad habit,
My one and only thought.
Leave me,
Please,
But stay.

Olivia Yvonne Bianco
Smithfield, KY

Waiting

Your son waits for you to get home,
long after you said you would arrive.
He longs for presents on his sixth birthday
and to feel your once loving embrace.
He wants you to say, "I love you," when he needs it most
and tuck him in when his eyelids grow heavy.

But, you won't be home.
You won't be there to feed him
or watch him grow.
You'll be in the company of killers,
breathing and addictive,
while he is in the company of
of…

You won't be the one to teach him right from wrong
or hold him when he cries.
For you are the reason his tears fall
on the nights he lies, waiting.

Katherine Elise Hamilton
Blue Springs, MO

Day of Painful Tears

The pane of pitter patter splash
Dripped across the slippery slope
Writing memories with transparent ink
Breathed upon with warm soft air

The reminiscence of the flow of time
Perfectly synchronized to the outpour of raindrops
Twirled the melody of childhood recollection
As I gently reclined in my white wooden rocking chair
Rhythmically moving back and forth
The sensual dance recreated my small dwelling place

Pausing to ponder, I sat in silence and closed my eyes
Slowly, I transcended into an alternate reality
A role reversed placed me in my small navy blue dress
Playing with my rag doll, staring at the window
While I stole glances at a tall plump figure
Whose face gleamed at me with a quiet smile
She wore grace on her hands
And strength on her fingertips
As they slowly knitted the silk blue thread on her lap

My grandmother aged with valor
She never wore the pain or suffering on her face
She wouldn't let me see
But I soon saw and felt what I could not understand
And knew for the first time
A pure love lost, my innocence distraught
For in a little while, she became submerged in my tears

Samantha Williams
Baltimore, MD

"Day of Painful Tears" was inspired by the desire to connect myself to an experience that was different from my own. I wanted to transcend my own individual experiences and utilize my imagination to bridge the gap of time between who I am and who I could have been. I also felt inclined to include an empathetic and nostalgic tone to the poem. I felt a familiar warmth and soft touch, as if the poem became my own memory. Essentially, I wanted to convey that I could deeply feel and understand an experience that wasn't fully mine.

Visions of Mundanity

Windowpane symphonies, spit and conducted in illogical mutterings
Amidst the humming anxiety and sweating, radiant rain beads
Transcendental trembling beneath the garish sheets
Treadmill-obsessed corpses, marbled fatty eyes
Spattering into the realm of that which we ramble not to think of
Wisconsin Avenue NW drenched, clenched shivers
Romanticism and tingling cigarillos break on the lips
Mournful sapphire feline irises
Glaring and soft and magnetic and unappealing
Mournful sapphire feline irises
Muttering to you in a hunched deer's tentative gaze
Piercing and fleeting in the polluted wood
Daily nearing expiration
Stretched buildings, purplish, bathed, elongated moonlit faces
Grinning slit in the cathedral wall
Choking on gelatin glass and projecting holy dentistry
Tattered leathery soles kicked up on the granite
Burnt orange coal in the steel belly of the garish serpent
In the temple of overwhelmingly snow-strained light
Reddened internal musician, pressed and stubbly, his cheap sunglasses
Shirtless and bulging, a swelled steak, futile and scathing
Microphone wire bruising his palms
All the acrid cigarettes
That elect cremation postmortem
That are content to be spread in picturesque mundanity
Guitar screams soul's contents through air, angelic sizzling gore
beaming

Raymond Clardy
McLean, VA

In my attempts to perfect an enhanced interpretive technique in which personal introspection and internalization are encouraged upon reading rather than literarily plodding towards an objective message, this product was developed. With a moderately abstract approach towards the articulation of mood, I attempted to express poetic thought through the recreation of unfettered and intense situational descriptions, both literal and semi-fantastical, climaxing into an aggravated and hallucinogenic narrative of redefined societal definitions and angst. I would like to thank Allen Ginsberg and denounce our public schooling system for their merciless repression of creativity and encouragement towards conformity and complacency.

The Night Hunt

Wake up! Wake up!
The hunt begins at night.
Yes! This night.
The hunters of the day have lost their right,
We begin at night.

Tonight,
Our prey will feel no fright,
Asleep, they'll feel no knife,
At night.
We begin at night.

Outside we go to await our prey,
We see it before a moment's delay.
We chase it, but it gets away.
Before me, the sky turns grey,
We'll have to wait another day.

Across the field, dawn alights,
We'll hunt again tomorrow night.

Meagan Elaine Tuvell
Live Oak, FL

Seven Billion

Close your eyes and empathize, recognize your compromise.
You idolize the crucified and circumcise the civilized.
You merchandise, industrialize, and privatize our school supplies.
You hypnotize to maximize, and multiply your enterprise.
Terrorized and traumatized, you'll mobilize the minimized.
You televise and fantasize to visualize this otherwise.
You can't disguise your own demise, that's self indulgent suicide.
So set our difference aside, and let me sneak my creed inside.
Take my sympathy inside you, understand me in regard to
7 billion little children playing your monopoly.
7 billion greedy children, spoiled children, needy children,
Unrewarding competition, keeps them from decomposition.
Passing kids and failing kids, domesticating invalids.
Loyal children, rebel children, appetitive egotism.
7 billion sycophants are living in significance.
7 billion psychopaths, escaping all the aftermath.
7 billion godly children, Christian children,
Muslim children, Jewish children, Hindu children,
Superficial superstition, contradicting contribution,
Stopping all our evolution.
"Lend your open mind to me, I'll give you a lobotomy,
Tuition is a guarantee that I'll supply the sodomy.
Bend your broken heart to me, I'll fill you with my prophecy,
Your faith is just your certainty on withering philosophy."

Jay Morris
Egg Harbor Township, NJ

Most humans possess existential anxiety somewhere in their minds. This fear develops into passive fantasy or active denial. As a result, complete cultural immersion prevails. This includes art, bigotry, faith, greed, militarism, nationalism, and many more aggressive means that appear to deny or escape death. When this aggression conflicts with that of another's, the most common of human suffering occurs. The majority of humans deny death and forsake life.

Another Restless Night

Another restless night,
So many restless nights I lie awake at night.
Can't seem to stop these thoughts,
These oh so many thoughts
Of things I can't make out but, they haunt me all the
Same I wish I knew these things.
I need to close these eyes
These oh so tired eyes just an ounce of sleep
Might help this man keep
All these thoughts at bay.
But that sleep seems so very far away.
It escapes this man every single night;
To think these things all night
Maybe just one night he might find his night.
But that night's not tonight it's just another restless night.

Anthony Randazzo
Rockford, IL

Cancer

So swiftly news came when they finally took the time
To hear the complaint and not just a whine
How quickly all changed in everyone's lives
When they finally realized that someone might die.

How galling the false words and sympathy appeared
For when the newness waned they all disappeared
So quickly you find who's really beside
As the time flies and treatments arrive.

How swiftly its presence sends cracks through the lines
That bind family, friends, and others beside
As temperaments flare in the face of unfair
For cancer does not discriminate or care.

It's easier to bury the feelings it brings
Than face the reality that fuels these things
And it hurts to be made to watch while they fight
When nothing you do will help them this time.

How often you wonder long into the night
Why cancer chose your loved one to fight
And why all the little things come into light
When nothing else can be all right.

Sarah Elizabeth Amundsen
Anchorage, AK

Four months ago, my family's lives were turned upside down when my mother was diagnosed with stage four brain cancer. She didn't present with typical symptoms, so the tumor was caught very late. Thankfully, the treatments have been successful so far. However, the road to get here has been hard and fraught with strife. My family has gone through a lot recently, and when I put pen to paper to write this work, I hoped to convey that.

Corruption

We live life without looking for answers
From history, we're not learning
Following patterns like dancers
Making money we aren't earning
Going corporate no returning

I'm not trying to promote hate
The purpose is to help you see
We shouldn't judge the outside trait
Let's live together it's our fate
We don't all have to agree

We're all different, and always will be
That doesn't mean we can't get along
The obvious that we hardly see
I won't quit on people I live among
I'm trying to teach, but I'm "too young"

This isn't a threat, it's a plan for peace
No wars, with pacifism we win
We can shortly see hatred decrease
A proof of that is Ghandi's major win
With racism we'll never see peace

Basil M. Elqasass
Buena Park, CA

Whistle in the Wind

On sunny days, the children play
On rainy days, the children pray
On gloomy days, I wander about,
Going in and going out
I walk into the bending woods
Fly away? I wish I could
A drop of rain hits my chin,
And all I hear is the whistle in the wind
The birds are chirping,
The fox is lurking
My hair now soaked with rain,
Helps to wash away all my pain
The ground turns to mud,
My clothes are dampened from this flood
Close my eyes, and breathe it all in,
Listen to the whistle in the wind
The trees are dripping with raindrops,
The sorrow is just all nonstop
Now the full moon has come out,
I'll take the longer route
All of the world has sinned,
So I'll just listen to the whistle in the wind

Maryn Margaret Jones
Midlothian, VA

Limbic System Production

If you could open the top of my cranium,
deep inside my eyes are like projector lenses
An upside down image of an angelic face,
on my left you should see all of my memory slides
Second to last shelf in alphabetical order lies
the short films of my daydreams
On my brain pod there should be trailers of
scenarios and wonders of her tendencies
On my right hangs a detailed mental picture of
her body and head shots
Vague snap chats of her poses,
along with priceless smiles in my memory vine
In the back of my mind lies an idea of a new memory,
but I just want her as my co-star
Then this could be my big memory picture
with previews of getting to hold her
Commercials of me being spontaneous,
episodes of us solving problems together
Special features of me surprising her for different holidays,
extras of us engaging in badinage
That's the end of the thought process,
if you would leave in a timely manner, I would appreciate it
I have food for thought being prepared as I think
These thoughts from the memory were brought
to you by Limbic System Production
A special thanks to a significant physical presence…

Lonnie Jones Jr.
Lake Charles, LA

Lies We Chose to Believe

I follow you because
gravity has its claws in all of us.
And I love you because
I don't know how to love myself.

Falling was like flying:
free, but
limited to the skies.
After all,
once you hit the ground,
you're not really falling anymore,
are you?

I listen to the silence because
its lies are so easy to believe when
something inside me whispers
much the same thing.

Drowning was like breathing:
free, but
only until I realized that
once you
fill your lungs with water,
you can't empty them
ever again.

Cassidy Buckland
Plymouth, IN

Reality Check

Life is not a fairy tale
I'm sorry for that, princess
If you need an example
I'll give you one for instance

I really hate to say it
But your wishes don't come true
No one knocks at your doorstep
To return a long-lost shoe

Cursed with awful ignorance
When born into good wealth
I'm sorry for you, princess
But learn to save yourself

Ashley Breann Vargo
Conroe, TX

The Two of Clubs

When you're playing poker
They always tell you to bet on face cards
But I drew the two of clubs
And ended up with a straight flush
And I could not care less about king and queens

Jacob Smith
Columbiana, AL

Untitled

My brain is a garden,
These damned thoughts are but seeds.
Why can I not grow flowers,
All I sew are weeds.
Push away all my desires,
For I am bound to another's needs.
I am told to follow life's rules,
And lie as my own heart bleeds.
They can't understand the strength of your rope,
In my life's fragile string of beads.

Aress Lynch
Hays, KS

The Flying Fugitive

It bit me.
Exactly one week ago.
But that's not the reason I hate it so.
I loathe it; not because it got its fill,
Nor invading my vein, or exacting that bloody pull.
I don't despite it stealing my blood,
But because my efforts, made me feel like: a dud.

That mosquito,
It made its haul as I lay in bed.
And then it hovered, tormenting my groggy head.
I twitched, at the nerve-racking sound I could not trace,
Before my own rebellious hand collided, with my face.

Following an abrupt end to my desire for sleep,
The lights were on.
Mosquito going, going, gone;
And I was left to weep.
Since then, I've hunted mosquitoes each vengeful day,
Murdered a thousand.
Still the single debt, I must repay.
As I lay deliberating the morrow's quest
Appearing from nowhere was the hounded pest.
With a brutal attack, I've ended the case.
I'm sure it's the one.
I recognize… the face.

Floyd J. Thomas
Hartford, CT

A Grandchild Remembers

Walking the chicken coops, sticks in our hands:
    an intriguing maze, an adventure land.
Five years and pigtailed and Grandpa, wise and tan:
    he taught me the art of tossing feed from a can.

And echoes of Grandma filtering through the corn stalks,
    to gather some mint, vining the fence 'long the walk,
peeling apples for cobbler, a breeze through her hair,
    she looks like Mother Nature with an apron to wear.

Being the oldest, I set the pace, but not far behind the others did race,
    thinking they were the first to find places to hide
    and discover their secrets and treasures with pride.

Years gone by, but each grandchild still thinks
    of the smell of fried chicken, the pump at the sink,
    where we rinsed off our hands and ran to the seat,
    of a board 'tween two chairs, swinging legs and small feet.

Walking the chicken coops, sticks in our hands.
    That tradition's passed on; it must be a plan,
    of *someone* much greater who knows that some parts,
    of our grandparents' lives, remain deep in our hearts.

Nancy Ann Dunn
Springfield, MO

Am I Beautiful?

Am I beautiful if I am skinny and my bones protrude out? I can eat whatever I want without gaining a pound. Hearing from everyone to eat more is a daily sound. Am I beautiful?

Am I beautiful now with a few extra pounds? Where the excess skin hangs over where my pants tie around. Hearing that I need to lose weight or there is never love to be found. Am I still beautiful?

Am I beautiful now with a full painted-on face. Using makeup to hide each imperfection I face. As I am chasing an unrealistic standard at a frightening pace: am I beautiful?

Am I beautiful now if I am poor and ashamed? I have nothing to give or a penny to my name. When I have nothing to show for, not even fame. Am I still beautiful?

Am I beautiful now in my own colored skin? Where there is no fight to be had, or race card to win. When you can actually see through the colors, sizes, and where I have been. Am I beautiful?

Am I beautiful now for the person I am? When you look at my heart and not what I physically am. With my inner beauty that shines brighter than any one object can. Yes. I am beautiful.

Erin Murray
Littleton, CO

Eating an Orange

Eating an orange to the fullest requires the use of all
five senses. When I eat an orange, I like to think about
everything I do. I grasp the orange feeling the smoothly rough
texture. While looking at the beautiful orange, I see little
craters. They remind me of lookin' at the moon through a
telescope. As I bring the orange close to my face, I can faintly
smell what's inside waiting to come out. It smells like it will
be sweet, which is good, because the last orange I ate was sour.
Curiously, I lick the outside of the orange wondering what it
will taste like. The only thing I taste is light bitterness.
Shaking the orange, I listen for something, but the only thing I
hear is the friction between my hand and the orange.

As I peel the orange, I can vaguely hear the skin tearing.
It sounds like a miniature zipper zipping, or a campfire
crackling. I can already smell the orange even though I haven't
finished peeling it. The scent is much stronger than it was
through the skin. Looking at the bare orange, I see thin, long,
white strands running throughout it like veins in our body.

While pulling the slices apart, the orange squirts juice in
the cut on my finger. It stings like a bee. When I take a bite,
I can feel all the little pieces of pulp bursting between my
teeth, filling my mouth with a wonderful, sweet, tangy taste.
When I am done, all I have left is some orange peel and the
memory of a great orange.

Jeff Hall
Melbourne, FL

A Moment of Time

If I could have just one thing in this world
I would just like a moment of time
To sit doing just about nothing
Writing things down on paper that rhyme

I would write about how great our world is to me
And of things I have seen in my life
I would write about how dark it gets with the night
And of how much we see when it's light

I would carefully place on my paper
All the words I could see in my mind
And when I've reached the last one I've written
I could look for more words for behind

With each sentence I write they're compounded
I've now paragraphs stretching for miles
At the ending of each word another
No ending quite yet but I smile

I so often have just thoughts to unravel
To write down while they're fresh in my mind
I could write some I'm sure of mind's travels
If I just had a moment of time

Michael Majewski
Three Lakes, WI

Growing Old Is a Blessing

Robert Browning wrote, "Grow old with me! The best is yet to be!"

In 1979, my dad printed this quote (a treasure) for my husband
and me;
It's hung on our wall all these years for everyone to see.

It makes us realize how precious God's gift of time is,
And that we should choose wisely the way we should live.

We enjoyed raising four children and now enjoy their families.
And as we grow older we feel blessed to have precious memories.

Just because of our age doesn't mean life's over yet.
Now we've got time to relax and enjoy our time that is left.

We should all appreciate and treasure God's gift of time—old
and new,
And we know that Robert Browning's quote really is true:

"Grow old with me! The best is yet to be!"

Enjoy God's gift of life.

Vonda and Bud Roberts
Wymore, NE

Milestones

Welcome adorable daughter of mine
You brighten my life like a beautiful song
And I'll spend every possible moment with you
Since you won't be a baby for long

Wake up my angel, it's your first day of school
And I wish I could be there beside you
But you'll make lots of friends, and you'll learn lots of things
From the teacher who'll be there to guide you

My! Don't you look pretty, my beautiful child
Why you're almost as tall as your mom
Your dress is so pretty; you're a vision for sure
And I know you'll have fun at your prom

Can't believe that you're leaving for college today
Tell me how have so many years passed
But I know that you're ready to be on your own
And these next years will go very fast

What a wonderful day for a wedding
All the plans and the guests are in place
And my heart tells me, too—it's the right thing for you
There's an aura of joy on your face

Welcome adorable grandchild of mine
You brighten my life like a beautiful song
And I'll spend every possible moment with you
Since you won't be a baby for long

Josephine Jenkins
Avondale Estates, GA

Recently, I celebrated my eighty-ninth birthday, and what a wonderful life it has been! Great health and a clear mind are my most valuable assets, but my greatest achievement has been raising seven beautiful, caring daughters who, in turn, became mothers themselves, raising children of their own. Together we experienced many individual milestones, each with its own special meaning. When combined, they created a patchwork quilt of beautiful memories for me. Since poetry has always been my way to memorialize people and events in a special way, I created "Milestones."

Walk with Me

I look at a bird,
and what do I see?
I really don't know,
it won't come to me.
My mind now,
is a blank slate.
It is just like the food,
you put on my plate.
My stomach growls,
I don't know what to do.
Forgot how to eat,
don't know how to chew.
I look at this man,
I have been with most of my life.
For a brief moment,
I know I am his wife.
Walk with me,
hold my hand.
Hold the one,
with the wedding band.
I thank you,
with all my heart.
For the vow you kept,
Til death do us part.
Walk with me.

Judith J. Hall
Maysville, GA

Acknowledge Yourself

When people don't treat you the way they should
And you're not feeling really good,
Turn on the music and stop the pain —
Discover the beauty of life again —
And acknowledge yourself.

When the world doesn't know just who you are,
Doesn't realize you are a star,
It's time to give up your worries and fears —
Just laugh at life and dry your tears,
And acknowledge yourself.

Talk to yourself,
And let yourself know
You are your own best friend.
Talk to yourself,
And feel yourself glow.
Good feelings have no end.

When a loved one isn't acting kind
And this indifference troubles your mind,
Pamper yourself and have some fun —
Look behind the clouds and see the sun —
And acknowledge yourself.

When you think that life has been unfair
And you want someone who really cares,
It's time to stop your harried pace.
Go to a mirror and smile at your face —
And acknowledge yourself!

Beverly Nader
Fairfield, CT

I love poetry and wrote my first poem when I was six years old. Though I haven't created a book of my poems, I'm a published author of several personal growth books and a speaker. I'm inspired by the many facets and aspects of personal and inspirational development, holistic health, and nature. My loving family includes three talented daughters and a granddaughter. My home overlooks about 170 acres of beautiful woodlands and I am inspired by these also. See more at www.beverlynadler.com.

A Tribute to Our Mama: Moments of Reflection

Mama, you were a wondrous gift
A bright and shining light,
That God gave to each of us
To teach us, wrong from right

Mama, you had a tender touch,
A cheerful, smiling face,
Just everything it took, to
Make our home a happy place

Mama, you had a gentle heart,
Whose willingness to share,
Could make our joys "seem" brighter still
Our pain less hard to bare

Mama, you were a wondrous gift
God gave us from above
To fill our days with warmth and joy
To fill our lives with love

Ralph King
Columbus, OH

I was born in Logan, West Virginia, in 1940 and graduated high school in 1960. I was voted class poet by 80% of the class. I had to write this piece anew to fit within the guidelines of the contest. I sat before a photograph of my mother and drew much inspiration from it, remembering all the things I thought she represented to us. Now that I've reached my seventies, I try to write a minimum of two poems a year.

For Jean Maurice, on Your Way to the Moon

You took my heart, when you slipped away
  Too suddenly, the other day
I've hugged your shirt, and cried the why
  To keep you close — won't say goodbye
You wouldn't say "leaving," when out the door
  You knew of returning, be back for more
Hugs, laughs, kisses, and smart remarks,
  I'll miss your smile, and miss your spark
I'll have you here, with me in ways
  That will be remembered, through every day
You've taken your body, left a piece of your soul
  Added to mine — to keep me whole
Thanks for your fire, of passion and hope
  Not only for me, for all in your scope
Your care extended, within many roles
  Will be missed and remembered, by many souls
Keep my heart with you, on your way to the moon
I'll keep you inside — til I see you soon

Michelle Bessette
Sarasota, FL

Until That Time

With the ever living life
That lives within me
I will never forget
The life that has moved on
For without you
The memory of you
Is always with me
For in my heart
You will always be
Together with the life of love
Is always the life of me
Until my time
I await the time
When I see you
Smiling once again
Right before me
I love you
I miss you
Until that time
I await the time
To be with you!

Samuel Kane Ortiz III
Albuquerque, NM

I am fifty-three years of age. In 2002, I lost my sister, Karen, to a battle with cancer; she was thirty-seven. On May 20, 2015, I lost my cousin Shawn to a battle with cancer; he was fifty. This poem is in memory of Shawn Montoya and my loving sister Karen M. Ortiz. I wrote this poem at 9:54 PM.

It's Beautiful, Lord

It's beautiful, Lord
  The sunset at evening
  The sunrise at dawn
  The birds in the springtime
  The moon when day is done
My heart thrills to see it
  I'm standing in awe
I'm thanking you, Lord
  It's beautiful

It's beautiful, Lord
  The snow falls in winter
  The colors of fall
The mountains and deserts
  The rush — of the falls
My mind can't conceive
  All your blessings on me
I'm thanking you, Lord
  They're beautiful

It's beautiful, Lord
The love that you gave
  Between woman and man
The smile of a baby
  The touch of her hand
The love of a mother
  The love of a friend
I'm thanking you, Lord, it's beautiful

Glendell Tilton
Shreveport, LA

Xenophobia

Altogether baffling concepts,
denying everything
future generations hold important.

Just keep learning
more now
of preposterous questions
resounding simple truths,
unimportant views.

Wicked xenophobia
yielding zephyr.

Ross A. Hawkins
Los Angeles, CA

Robert Pinsky (born October 20, 1940) served as Poet Laureate Consultant in Poetry to the Library of Congress from 1997 to 2000. Among his poetry works is "ABC," a poem whereby Pinsky challenged himself to write a poem with the first letter of each progressive word lists the alphabet in order. I accepted the same challenge and created "Xenophobia."

No Turning Back

Yesterday was a day of baffled thoughts
Confusion in infinite corners
Twisting and turning
No turning back
Just dragging ahead
Numerous morals to master
Not enough time
Countless emotions flooding my system
Only making it harder to realize which are true
And which are false

Today
Today is quite a day
Yet not just any day
A day which happens once and only once
Must savor the present
Because there's
No turning back
Just racing ahead
To reach

Tomorrow
Tomorrow is filled with wonders
Tomorrow will be sprinkled with magic
No indications of tomorrow's discoveries
Just opportunities for a fresh new start
Tomorrow will smell of delighted hearts
Tomorrow will taste of sweetened sugar plums
Yet always enjoy the now
Because whereas darkness may find you
Sooner or later
At this moment you can find light
And to you
It will come

Julia Kiusals
Palatine, IL

I Did Not Know

I did not know my daughter was abused by her spouse.
I did not know the bruises on her arms were caused by
frequent beatings.
I did not know she wore long sleeves on a hot day to hide the
bruises from physical abuse.
I did not know when he screamed and called her names at the
family dinner table, that was verbal abuse.
I did not know when he took the money that she earned, that
was financial abuse.
I did not know when he told her to give up medical school
and her education, that was intellectual and educational abuse.
I did not know when she told me he had threatened to kill her
that he would do it.
My eyes did not see the turmoil, the anguish, the pain.
My ears did not hear the tortured screams for help.
When I asked if everything was okay, she simply said, "Yes Mom,
everything is fine."
It was easier to believe "everything is all right."
He threatened to kill her, but now she said,
"Everything is fine." "It must be all right,
Maybe it was just a misunderstanding."
What I do know now, my child is dead.
My voice was not heard while she was alive,
Because I was silent.

Lanalee J. Campbell Leonard
St. Thomas, VI

I Wonder

I wonder what makes the grass so green,
and the trees grow straight and tall.
I wonder what makes the stars so bright,
and sometimes not seen at all.

I wonder what makes the ocean roar,
and the ebb and flow of the tide,
and the cold, cold winds that blow from the north,
and nature's creatures all trying to hide.

I wonder what makes the mountaintops,
their majestic peaks surveying the land.
I wonder what makes the forest so full,
and the desert nothing but sand.

I wonder what makes the river flow,
as it winds around the bend.
I wonder what lies beyond the skies,
in the heavens that never end.

I wonder…

Walter E. Clayton
New Brighton, PA

Wally Clayton was born in Alliance, OH, and graduated from Rochester High School in PA. He served as sergeant in the US Air Force from 1946 to 1949. He retired as a mail carrier for the US Postal Service in Beaver, PA. He became known as "Tacky the Clown," making animal balloons and a little magic. He is director of "Men of Melody" that entertain at organizations, churches and nursing homes. He has two published poems, "Mother's Day" and "Layman's Prayer," and wrote and recorded one song in Nashville, TN: "Tears I Cannot Hide." He has a wife, Eleanor, children: Dian, Harry, Paul, David, and many grandchildren and great-grandchildren.

Strike Out!

If smokers knew how much they stunk,
They would be in such a funk.
Careful if you hug a smoker,
You will smell like you play poker.
So please, if you can,
Kick the habit, make a plan!

Barbara Swanson
Washington, DC

The Day I Lost You

I remember when I was little and the sound of your voice
comforted me so much.
Maybe it was the look in your eyes, or your soft gentle touch.
You told me you loved me and would never leave my side,
But time after time, you always lied.
I wanted to be with you, and wanted you to be with me,
But that was never enough for you to see reality.
I thought of you a lot, cried for you every night,
Hoping God would hold you tight.
I prayed for change, but nothing came.
I prayed for change, but felt only pain.
I hope one day you'll come back to me,
And be the mom you were meant to be.

Samantha Velez
South San Francisco, CA

He's a Hurricane

Can we take a moment to talk about your eyes
they could be any color and still remind me of skies
Skies of blue and skies of grey, skies you could
look into once and be lost all day
And your hair—like the waves in the sea
swooping and dancing, just smiling at me
Your skin like the valleys, light and plain
the simplicity and the glory—a contrast you can't explain
And your hands, rough with years of pain
still kind and reaching out, so jealous of
your fingers as they carelessly play about
tracing your lips, sweeping through your hair
as I sit here deciding whether I wish you'd catch my stare
Maybe it'd be good
Maybe your oceans would reach my swamps, puddles
and ponds
Maybe your valleys would touch my mountains,
my ditches, my craters
And isn't it a tragedy that the boy I see
is a floodlight and he thinks he's just a lit match
And isn't it sad that this great catch sees himself
as a drip, when he's actually a hurricane

Maya Durham
Kissimmee, FL

My name is Maya Pearl Durham. I am fourteen years old. I've grown up in a small, woodland community… with the life of the party as a mom and an English major, musician, and misanthrope as a daddy… They're amazing people. I've learned the importance and power of words; I choose each one carefully. I love that I can be so emotional and passionate and then I just leave it on the page. I hope my writing makes you feel something, strongly. Any emotion will do.

The Lack of Compromise

I push my soul, I try again
To reach the top, to charge the summit
I fear for man, it is a sin
To shun the task, or to shy from it

Sail your ship from pole to pole
And should the wind cease to gust
Set the oars and begin to row
The challenge is there, succeed you must

We possess a strength to conquer all
In our rebellious but reverent spirit
Failed has the man, before the summit, shall fall
But is satisfied to have been near it

Show no fear in the dark hours of life
You have an eternal light
Stand your ground, your head held high
And walk by faith, not sight

When you feel too worn to go the length
But you will not be denied
And you wonder where you get the strength
It's the lack of compromise

William Lee Hancock
McAlester, OK

The Odyssey of Life

I went through strife every night,
and just turned off the light.
No fight, no fight, they yelled with might.

It lit this light,
that ignites me with the power to fight.
But she yelled at me: "Not tonight."
And I decided not to bite.

These twists, these turns,
They make me burn.
I yearn for her.

It was my fault, not hers!
On our trip in the ship
They yelled, "All aboard,"
Yet she went overboard.
I promise you, I deplored.

You're gone, I miss you.
How could I do this to you?

I owe a great debt,
But I'm yet to repay that debt.

So here we are, at the end of these prison bars,
At the end of our odyssey.

I'll miss you, baby.

Samantha Jones
Burbank, CA

Uncertainty

I knew from the
beginning that you
were just a flirt.
And yet I fell in love
with you knowing I'd
be hurt.
I thought that I could tie
you down and make
you love just one,
but how could I do
something no one else
has ever done.
I know you'll never love me
and I'm trying not to cry, for
I must find the strength to
kiss your lips goodbye.
So when you look for
me again you'll find
I won't be there,
I want a love to call
my own not one I'd
have to share. So I
will hide my broken
heart beneath a laughing
face, and though you
think I never cared
no one else could take
your place.

Deborah Curlew McAleer
Mastic, NY

His Worn Rattan Chair

Whence it came, I do not know
But now it sits upon the snow
He steps outside to get away
From the troubled thoughts
That cloud his day
Mango Tango may be a part
That is reaching into his heart
While he sits and contemplates
The many things he may hate
I hope he finds some love
That I can take care of
He is a mystery man
Thinking he has a plan
But deep inside that beautiful soul
He may feel he's in a fish bowl
Swimming through emotions, fighting the tide
Maybe feeling he has to hide
Come out and express
What you may feel is a mess
Sit by the fire and aspire
Your true self that I admire
It may seem like a struggle
To go through a muddle…
If you feel me in you
Then your days will be true

Carol Shute
Mattapoisett, MA

Illusive Is This Thing

Illusive is this thing
Of reflection and promise.
To immerse in it is
A construction of love.

Molded focus and labored tiers
Usher gradual hopes and fears.
A slow awakening unfolds
As vulnerability's exposed.

While tailored wisdom is honed
With each pause at rejection,
Drudgery's toils and missteps
Breed calloused resolve and depth.

Wrestling then, 'til reaching there
The first door... where

The casting call — the call back,
The editor's note — the contract,
The interested gallery — the show,
My wait! The wait to know...

I am an actor. I am a writer.
I am an artist.
I... am a star.

Elated leaps bring tears of joy.
Illusive, this thing,
For tomorrow it brings...

Rejena Bennett
Stamford, CT

Never Truly Gone

When you lose a loved one
They haven't gone away,
As one of God's angels
They walk beside you every day.

Their presence surrounds you
Unseen, unheard but always near,
Forever in your heart
Still loved, still missed and very dear.

All the cherished memories
You can reflect upon,
Will keep the spirit alive
Of those who have gone.

They'll live in your heart
Until you meet again,
With your angel always nearby
Watching over you, amen.

Dorothy Baboo
South Amboy, NJ

Thanks for My Spouse

You were blessed into my life. You don't realize how much you are appreciated or how much you give of yourself to others. I appreciate the husband and father you are.

Chorus:
Thanks for my spouse. I'm really thanking you—the man above. You brought so much into our lives—this bond of love. And believe you me I'll never let you go.

The love I have for you is the love I have in me. I'll stand and watch you with the kids. I always want to run in and interrupt the play. I just want to hug and kiss you. With you right here with me, I'll have the strength to go on.

Chorus:
Thanks for my spouse. I'm really thanking you the man above. You brought so much into our lives—this bond of love. You walk into my arms—I'll hold you close to me. And believe you me—I'll never let you go. You are the definition of the word father. And the superlative of all husbands. You look and act, just like a little boy, when you frolic with them. You're so overwhelmed in playing you look so cute.

Chorus:
Thanks for my spouse. It is always such a beautiful sight to watch you frolic with them. And believe you me I'll never let you go. The love I have for you, is the love I have in me.

Tujuanna Benson
Montgomery, AL

Family

I have family here
I have family there
It seems I have family everywhere
Some are near,
Some are far
It matters not
I love them all
Wherever they are
Such a wonderful gift
they are to me
I have been blessed
So lovingly,
With a family who cares
As much as they do
Although the Lord
Has called some away
I love and think of them
Each and every day
My beautiful family
You're the best
Anyone could hope for
I know you will always
Catch me if I should fall
Now and forever
I thank you
God bless you all

Karen T. Hall
Six Mile Run, PA

I am very grateful to everyone responsible for the opportunity of having my poem entered into a contest. My wonderful family inspired my poem. I've enjoyed reading and writing poetry all my life. Now, I would like to tell you a little about myself. I was born in Norristown, PA. I now reside in Six Mile Run, a small town in Pennsylvania. I've been married forty years. I have four children and nine grandchildren. I look forward to writing more poetry in the future. Thank you.

All Hallows' Eve

Brightly-hued autumn passing into the cold darkness of winter
Summer's sunny, breezy lightness fading into the grey seriousness
   of autumn
Leaves once bursting with color, crumpled and withered,
Blown to the ground by the chilling winds
Darkness comes much earlier now
Hordes of bright orange jack-o'-lanterns interrupting the
   blackness of night
Only the moon can illuminate with its cold brightness
Real monsters lurking in the shadows, while pretenders roam
   the streets
Threatening tricks, if denied the customary treats
Kaleidoscopic leaves at the peak of their brilliance
Representing autumn at its spectacular zenith
Rapidly fading into the bleakness of bitter winter

Christy Armentrout
Charleston, WV

Old Friend

I know it's not right, to feel the way I do,
Especially since you knowingly, broke my heart in two.
Through all moments of the day, I see you, wherever I go.
Wishing you held my hand, as my heart beats oh so slow.
For it is you that holds the key to my heart,
Even though, we are now worlds apart.
I wish we would have had a chance to be something great,
However, this seems to not be a part of our destiny or fate.
Apart we must learn to love and grow again,
How I miss the days when I could call you "as friend."
I hope you are happy and contented with the life you lead.
Just know, that deep in my being, my heart for you, still bleeds.
I put on a pleasant smile, masking the hurt that stays.
I wonder if I will ever stop counting the days,
Until I see you again, God only knows.
But you hold my heart, wherever I may go.
I know it's wrong to feel how I do.
However far, however long, I will always care about you.

Corrissa Williams
Tacoma, WA

Because of Ms. J. K. Rowling and my dear friend, P. M. B., I have tapped into a talent that I never thought was possible. She inspired me to be comfortable with my writing, and he inspired me to always follow my dreams, whether they are made of magic or even copper pipes! Writing is my release and my passion. Embrace what you love, as I have done. Thank you!

Yellow Eyes

Never walk in the woods alone
Where at night the trees seem to moan and groan
The black night is lightless with stars covered by gray, wispy clouds
I am not afraid
The long arms of the trees reach for me
The branches crack, but the sound comes from the top of the tree

I am not afraid
From the top of the tree, two luminescent eyes appear
This could prove to be my biggest fear
The wind sends a shiver down my spine
The yellow eyes seem to sway like a vine
I am not afraid

They descend down the tree in a stalking manner
The tree sways in the wind like a banner
I step back
The light bulb eyes seem to not want to attack
The moon breaks through and I am thankful for that
The moonlight reveals the silhouette of a Siamese cat

KarLee McNeel
Pheba, MS

I Know There Is a God

I know there is a God
Because He is the only one who counts the tears my soul cries
When my body and mind are numb
From the barbs of enemies and swords of friends.

I know there is a God
Because when I finally break the surface
Of my pain, gasping for understanding
To breathe humanity back into my being,
He throws me a lifeline and tows me to a place without judgment.

I know there is a God
Because when the elevator shoots to the top floor,
Butterflies churning, blood turned to bubbling adrenaline,
He meets me in the stars, and never pushes the down button.

I know there is a God
For I have faced darkness that doesn't promise a sunrise at dawn,
And I have lost pieces of me to that eternal blackness
But remained whole, assured there was a torch burning just beyond.

I know there is a God
For unworthy of the slightest reward for last-place in the human race
He gave me the most precious of trophies to coach to victory:
Slowing steps, seeing faces, filling needs like potholes in a track,
Above all, showing people she knows there is a God.

Cindi Griggs Rockwell
Elizabethtown, PA

Icy Breath

I am graceful
    I am beautiful
    I am slow to come
    I am lonely

I chase my friend Summer;
she is fast like lightning in midday's storms.
I never seem to catch up;
like a wave that never seems to meet the shore.
I waste the days away blowing my icy breath on unexpected visitors.

Because, you see, I am lonely like the first star in the night sky.
My heart is as stiff and cold as a rock:
falling into a river of doubt.

        I am Winter.

Alison Grace Hall
Columbia, MO

This Must Be Love

You've had my attention
Since we first met.
You've kept me at my best,
Even when I had all the reasons in the world
To be at my worst.
You've never given up on me,
Even when I gave up on myself.
You made me feel like life was worth living,
Like eventually everything would work out,
Even when everything was falling apart.
When I was younger,
I would never have been able to understand
What these feelings meant.
But as I grew more and more,
It finally hit me.
It's love.
I love you.

Angelique Ann Marie Buffum
Pensacola, FL

The End It Knows Well

A beast in the chasm of art that rumbles and ruptures
Pretty pieces and placid scenes
Not knowing exactly where to
Start
But the end, it knows well
Filled is its little finger with enough sorrow to cripple
A thousand men, yet it thinks of breathing as
Swell
Tell God what you have seen,
That his creations are a devastation to the sweetness
Of everywhere and nowhere that anyone has ever
Been
What does it know, really?
Of kindness, of empathy, of all its horrors and wreckage?
Slightly, not quite enough,
But maybe one day it will understand the beauty of a
Lily
The value of a naked palm, disclosed fleshy fingers
Warm, warm crimson blood pulsing beneath skin
Woven with intentions as pure as a swell act,
Which when ceased to be practiced by it
Will bless every stretch of the earth with undeniable
Calm

Lauren Ellyse Ewald
Jasper, AB

Candy-Coated Solitude

Caramel dreams,
candy-coated screams,
cotton candy clarity,
and Coke
bottle blues.

Smoke swollen with sorrow,
savoring secret solitude.
Melting matter mindlessly
underneath.

Who are you?

Bittersweet candy girl,
spiked with salt and sulphur.
A pure white devil,
who desires to live harder.

Comfortably ignorant,
yet tainted with truth.
Bound by heaven's blood forever,
I will not lose you.

Naomi Rocca
Victoria, BC

*This poem was written for a class assignment twenty-eight years ago;
I was eighteen. I still have the sheet of paper it was first penned on, now
yellowed and frayed. I've kept it as a reminder of the first time I felt my
voice come through on a page. It was inspired by my sister's struggle and
how I could relate. This is my first submission to be published because
the message, unlike the page, will never age.*

My Cocoon

Short steps take, and take
                    And take
                        Are you lonely? She's said just afraid
                    No one but sure gleefully
He's aware
Oh but sure as conceivably said
                        I'm here, billows of smoke
            At that point nothing
                Do you want to come over to say...
Oh? How she tried looks him in the eye and asserts
Truly, she's dropping the line he's
                    Much so much to you
                    O! It isn't a sure likeness
                    Clandestine!
        She says close the door
Where would you have me go? I'm so afraid she says
All the world's a stage
Mr. he motions to her chaise lounge, and
What these people are expressing is their tardiness and irrelevance
Like
                            Si A Nari

Drake Dudley Richardson
New York City, NY

The March of Time

I walked along a lonely lane,
A pale moon overhead.
Cast eerie shadows 'cross my path,
I followed where it led.
No human noises could I hear.
No sulfur filled the air.
Before me loomed an ancient ruin,
I sat and lingered there.

I thought about these crumbling walls,
Built centuries long gone by.
And of the men who built these walls,
They lived like you and I.
They lived their lives and dreamed their dreams,
They loved, they fought, they died.
But now of them all that remains,
These old walls by my side.

As I am now so too were they,
As they are I will be.
All I have is this moment,
Of morn' no guarantee.
I'll help my neighbor while I can,
And cease to question why.
Soon someone, some one else by grass grown mound,
Will wonder, who was I.

Thomas Cantwell
Miramichi, NB

Mirror

I boil beneath her gaze, festering like a sore
Engulfed in flames, a pain I ignore.

Her eyes undress me, revealing what I hide
The secrets I have guarded, the tears I have cried.

She is cruel, in the way she sees,
Picking apart my serenity,
Hoisting me up, like strange fruit on a tree.

My skin scarred, like dirt in fresh snow.
I smell the burning of flesh, that I recognize as my own.

I swing back and forth, controlled by the wind,
As she whispers the weaknesses I hold within.

She cuts me down, when I've accepted defeat.
My head hangs low, like the branches of a tree.

I wouldn't dare look up, to behold my enemy.
With one look in the mirror
I recognize her as me.

Taylor Bianca Darks
Cincinnati, OH

Life Story

I am trapped inside a cage:
Every page
Written by someone who doesn't know
Me.
Every chapter,
Every scene,
Stars someone else —
Something less —
While I am a footnote,
Only to give reference to
The *when*, *where* and *how*.

Terese Mason Pierre
Toronto, ON

The Sea Animal's Empty Home

The sea animal's empty home is
More beautiful than mine,
More studied than an architect's design,
More elaborate than a turreted castle.

I would crawl into this empty shell,
To live my life at the sea bottom,
Protected by my mother ocean,
Floating in peace within the bosom of life.

Barbara A. Martzen
Turlock, CA

Men of Valor

These men so brave and bold
Their story is still not fully told.
Of how knee deep in the silt,
They died face down, but not to wilt.
The memory of these valorous men
Shall always be remembered until then.

To those who returned not fully whole,
But who stayed in their slimy trenches like a mole
Until God and man called, up and over they crept
To conquer the enemy and save those of us who wept.
To all the living and the dead who saved our democracy,
We bow in reverence, pride and humility.

Marilyn Nellie Grace Brewster
Stilesville, NB

*Having been born in 1942 near the end of World War II, I became so aware of
the men and women in our community who had so valiantly given their lives
to keep us free. In high school I began to write essays and poetry which allowed
me to express my heart's passion about the world around me. It brought to
my remembrance the many years before, standing at the Remembrance Day
ceremonies in our community, as we solemnly gave honor to our veterans.
These memories led me to write "Men of Valor." I so wanted to individually
honor our service men. After all these years to have the opportunity to publicly
share this poem is such a God-given blessing to me!*

Our Love Will Last Forever

I knew when I saw you it was good
The light of my love and good to my eye
The bearer of my soul and the keeper of my heart
The love of my life and the oh my, oh my
You have been there through many things
The hurts, the bad, the ugly and the joy
The ups and downs, the tears and the smiles
I knew you would not my heart destroy
I have loved you through thick and thin
For you have held me tight with loving hands
My heart grows stronger day by day
Knowing you are there to my every demand
You have been my hands and my eyes
My ears, my feet and my all in all
You are my love the first and the last
You are my strength, my eternal wall
I love you now as I did years past
It will be here no matter how long
For my heart belongs to only you
For God has placed me where I belong
Dear God thank you for giving me love
Thank you for letting it last so long
Please let it continue forever Lord
And let this be my eternal song

Yolanda W. Porter
Mobile, AL

Day and Night

The paradigm of youth unfurled at the fist,
Then clenched back up around the fat of my breast

So there it is,
The contents of my life's bliss
Splattered on the walls of an empty abyss
Ahh so there it is,
The contents of a lover's journal
They lied,
Someone told me we were born eternal

And if the sun hid in fear,
Would the world move slower,
And could I finally tear

Calm me,
Please,
And by morning let it fall,
Dragged by the ankles of my shadow,
A pain to enthrall
Keep me hollow,
At least my ignorance will hold companionship,
Oh what a championship

So let sleep come,
Come as a coma
Lay rest to my sullen fury,
And let die both judge and jury

Chitra Amba Nidadavolu
Trumbull, CT

The List

There is a list
We are all on
We don't know when
We'll be called upon
It could be today, tomorrow, or the next
But if you're not ready, you could be perplexed
You must live everyday
As though it is your last…
'Cause it just may be…
And the consequences are vast
Have you said I love you daily
To the ones you love?
Have you accepted Jesus Christ
As your personal savior from above?
When you leave this life
Will your loved ones rest assured
Knowing that all you were ailing from
Has been spiritually cured?
So you better double check
Be sure there is nothing you've missed
Only you can guarantee that
You are on "the list"!

Tina L. Perna
McComb, MS

Don't Cry

The tears rolling down your face
They seem as if they can't be stopped
It seems as though nothing is in their way
But what good does it do you to show those trickling streams
They only carve away at your already broken heart
And leave a long scar
You don't need to carry that scar
You don't need to lose to the pain
You don't need to cry
You don't need those tears
Save them for later when you'll really need them
But now is not the time to call them out
For now, just keep them in
Hide them, don't show them to the cold world
There's no need to show them
No need to cry baby
So don't cry

Jenny Kim
Baton Rouge, LA

Shadows

There are these shadows
Following everyone around
Everywhere we go, yet they don't make a sound
They don't have a face
They don't have a name
But they are empty and faceless, just the same
But what is their aim?
These shadows that lurk around every corner
Are they to remind us of the mistakes we've made?
The pain we've caused?
The names we've slain?
Are these shadows merely a ghost of the past?
Or a dark reminder of what not to do in the future?
Whatever their purpose, there they remain
Attached at the hip
Dragging us down in chains
These shadows are a mystery
Not because they are a dark oil stain
But because we fear what they might contain

Marisa J. Recker
Anacortes, WA

I am fifteen years old, and I am from Anacortes, Washington. I have always wanted to be a writer. I want to spread my words to others, and I desire to inspire those who read my work. My dream is to be a successful author and to make my readers feel something when they read my words. This poem was inspired by the things in life that hold us back from following our dreams: shadows, if you will. I hope to inspire others to break free of their shadows and follow their dreams.

The Life of a Book

Isn't it funny how life is like a story
And how some lives are gory.
Some people who have friends,
Yet some who don't even get to begin.
With our books small in chapters
Yet we can still find laughter,
But what about the book that ends sad?
When all we cared about was what ended glad.
What about the character who died?
All because they listened to the whisper lies,
And what about the boy who fell?
Did we read what he had to tell?
What about the teen who would fly?
Did we care at all she would cry?
We calm these things but we don't listen,
Some people just smile and pretend.
So what about the book that is you?
Do you hope people will read through?

Jamie C. Jenkins
Ontairo, CA

I am a junior at School of Arts and Enterprise. I am the youngest out of five family members. I'd like to take a moment and thank my brother, Casey, for serving in the Marines. My thought process behind this poem began when I realized I didn't like sad endings in books. Then I began to think these books could relate to lives of other people that no one has met yet. And thus came to life my poem to bring forth my discovery.

Pain

Some hide their pain,
deep where no one can ever get to it.
While, others embrace their pain.
They wear it on their sleeves,
hoping that you will take it away.
I want to take your pain.
I never again want to see your beauty contoured with pain.
I want your life to be full of happiness,
so full that no one can ever take it away.
Give your pain to me.
Hide it away with mine,
so no one can ever get to it.
Even you will never find your pain.
Our pain is my burden.

Michele Lauren Moran
Ronkonkoma, NY

Chasing Dreams

One night you have a dream,
You feel that it could be done someday,
When you wake up in the morning,
And think, no, this has to be done,
This dream I had.

Days, weeks, months pass by,
The world still rotates the same way,
You still have little hope
That this dream will be found someday,
This dream I had.

Years pass by,
And you cling onto your shred of hope for success,
I have finally found what I'm looking for!
It was always right here in my soul!
This dream I had!

How happy you are, that happiness you have,
Makes you dream good dreams that night,
When you find another dream to chase,
The same story repeats again,
This dream I had.

Sravani Viswanadha
Cupertino, CA

I am a seventh-grade girl from Cupertino, CA. In our literature class, we were asked to write a poem on some topic, and I chose "Chasing Dreams." When we dream a good dream, instead of waiting for it to occur in the real world, we can try and find it. But in the end, we realize it's inside us — it's what we see, feel or think. When I shared these thoughts through the poem with my family and friends, I got enormous support and encouragement. Then I decided to share my poem with a wider audience.

Predators

Can we sense the predators in our midst?
Can we pretend that they don't exist?
Is that what makes us the prey?
Hoping we're not being hunted day to day
Trying to act natural as they creep up on you
Trying to find a way to use yourself against you
To gain your trust and watch you lose
They hold your hand as you tie your noose
Blindsided and vulnerable they're ready to hit
They throw it all in your face with their venomous spit
Tear you down as if you didn't matter
Watch you break down, watch you shatter
With an insatiable vacancy still harboring inside
The fire still burns, it is still very much alive
Never enough you will never be free
They will never release their awful decree
For they are the victim in this terrible game
You have wronged them, you should be ashamed
Projection is the predator's little trick
Make everyone believe they are the weak and the sick
Escape the moment or succumb to the madness
Every shred of dignity is engulfed with sadness
Projection is now reflection, an image so distorted
A simple missing person who's never reported
Run away or stay and pay the ultimate cost
Breathe fire with the dragon and you'll be forever lost

Rachael Lee Rice
Anaheim, CA

Love Is a Verb

Love is a verb,
so much power in a single word,
the power to pull someone out of dark solitude
and the power to turn someone into a moon;
It can heal pain within a single flick
when you say it to me it happens rather quick.
My voice trembles and shakes like a leaf,
I only wish to give you that same relief,
so I'll be your support, your shelter from the storm
and when things turn cold my arms will keep you warm.
For your demons don't scare me, I have my own
and despite the distance my words could be a home
for you, so that you could have a safe place
and so I'll have an excuse to see your beautiful face.
If words could build bridges and my soul was a plane
I'd drop everything and rush to you at the sound of my name;
so there would not be a need of yours that I would not provide,
and if you ever sent me away, I swear I will abide,
because love is a verb
and I'll keep every word.
My love won't be bound by verbal expectations.
I swear to show it to you, even across the nations,
it's the very least I can do
for being so deeply in love with you.

Hannah Marie Davis
Valdese, NC

The Last Call

I call all my loved ones to say my last good-byes
I know I'm not going to make it out alive
I hear panic in my voice
I feel my hands tremble as I hang up the telephone
I hear a loud bang as it hits the desk
I glance out the window
I can't see anything besides flames and smoke
My heart is pounding inside of my chest
I feel my throat closing up
My breath starts to shorten
Suffocating, I frantically look around to try and find a way out
The only way out is down
I take a leap of faith and jump out the window
As I fall to my death I pray for peace
For my loved ones will be sure to feel grief

Rachel Kaye Amburgey
Huntington Beach, CA

Stunted Growth

Growing up is weird
You continue to repeat the same habits as you did as a child
Except things are slightly different
Gum packets become cigarettes
Sugar highs become drug highs
You might meet a boy with green eyes that sparkle with mystery
He will have the softest olive skin,
You will want to rub against your porcelain body
He has a different type of cooties now, STDs and heartbreak
When he rips away you might feel a gap that was once filled with joy
You'll take a trip to get away
Not in a story book with the narrating of your mother's soft voice
You'll walk to a bar,
Try to fill the emptiness
With as many shots of Jack Daniels as you can
When you were a kid you heard of a girl with the long brown hair,
Crying over the freshly scraped knees
Sitting on the blood stained cement
Instead of a bike she tries something new
She tries to love
Instead of scraped knees
She now has scraped wrists and a cracked heart
You see, growing up is weird
We have the same habits as we did when we were younger
But the moral behind them is slightly different—
Instead of doing things to enjoy life
We do it to kill a little monster called Pain

Margaret Vivian Pellegrom
Spring Lake, MI

*I just turned eighteen, and I wrote this poem a year after my recovery from
severe depression. During my journey I noticed a lot of things. One: everyone has
monsters in their head and skeletons in their closets. I also learned that people
will pretty much do anything to cope and keep their skeletons hidden and their
monsters mute. The real moral behind my poem is that love can be either one of
the most beautiful feelings or the worst.*

Tortured Soul

Consumed by pain that won't let me be
surrounded by fools whom cannot see
Pushed ahead by pain by pain that will never be gone
filled with rage, not sure I want to go on
I'm filled with pain, this can't be wrong
Why do these demons torture me,
I look around, can no one see?
I scream in pain, this can't be fair,
my tortured soul, this pain laid bare.
I tried to speak but no one would hear,
with this shattered mind, I'm filled with tears
Hounded by dreams of what once was real
consumed by pain, I don't want to feel
Why won't the memories go away
how much longer, do I have to pay
My mind and soul were shattered by rape,
hounded by pain, there's no escape
The needles and lines numb my brain,
the agonizing memories drive me insane
What was this for why did it happen?
I still remember how he stood there laughing
No one would listen no one would hear
no one can see how my soul's been seared
Why did he do it, can't he feel?
For the rest of my life these things I'll feel
Next time people don't look away
for if you do more of us will pay

Angelique Noire
Sanfrancisco, CA

Darkness

The fear in your eyes is just a lie,
For you know in your head you'll cry.
You try so hard to forget,
But it's there like a reminder on replay.
People tell you it's okay,
But we all know what's fake.

Lindsey Jae Vandieren
California, MO

A Personal Kind of Currency

My jewel encrusted tongue is paved in treasure
Opal, emerald, amethyst and more
My mouth can molt these riches at my leisure
These golden keys unlock what I adore

It's in the way the words are strung together
Making more a necklace than a line
Which in bedazzled language strangles never
The throat that strings the diamonds and is mine

As eloquence and glamour do distract
I beautifully conquer all that I attract

Lindsey Ryan
San Diego, CA

Jessica

Does your disease bring you closer to God?
Do you count the bumps on your rosary bead spine,
Twist your neck like one possessed
To see your shoulder blades fan out
Like the wings of an angel?
And have you been exorcised?
Or does the blood on your knuckles still make you feel
Alive?
The way it dribbles down your translucent skin
Like sacramental wine into glass
And with every hair you shed,
You must be getting a little bit lighter
Maybe one day you can disappear altogether
But today, there is work to be done
Because there is such thing as a perfect body,
And it is yours to have any way you choose,
Isn't it?
And you choose the violent jut of your hip bones
The gap between your thighs
The splay of your collarbones
Against waxy skin
Like the embedded wicks of the candles
On your altar
But it was never really about size for you, was it?
You just wanted your bones to show so they would finally see
Everything that was inside of you

Katya Melissa Zinn
Pasadena, CA

Admiration of Art

Please do not fly impatiently overseas
without my heart, wrapped safe and tight, on the same ride.
I'll be forced to live caged, trapped by hostel room keys.
Scuffed while you grow scruff, only with you I'll abide.

Do not take your time with French ladies, whose frowns
form addictions with the allure of listlessness.
The distinguished Dutch and English, with their gold crowns
bejeweled, will try to outshine my mute fondness.

But you will look at Venus de Milo and see
the capsuled body that resembles my fixed heart.
Your applause for her is a melody to me.

I will wait in your suitcase while you admire art.
Mona Lisa's beauty has you thinking, again,
of me. You toss a wish into Trevi Fountain.

Jaylene Acheson
Delta, BC

Curiosity

My skin becomes the floor and my eyes become the walls
I'm trapped inside a space with no way to run, no maze to solve
My fingertips trace pathways, between the dotted lines
I cannot seem to find a way to break the patterned tiles
My eyelashes flicker as they stare down the sun
A sun coated in blank white ceiling, covered by curtains and a rug
The doe-eyed morning droplets blinking up from the green floor
Sway in time, to the rhyme, that makes up this prison block
No escape is necessary when you are imprisoned for no crime
It's simply the lack of rules that form bars unchanged by time
The laws that do appear, the things that do make sense
Only serve to set off the confusion of the rest
And it is this that makes us question
And this that torments us unsolved
As empty holes and voided questions
Enthrall with iron claws
We cannot escape the pull, you see
The *gravity*, you might say,
Of the stone-hearted unbending hatred
Of ever-loved curiosity
And in the end you'll seem to find
That those things which do make sense
The turning of the earth, or the force which keeps us bent
Simply cause more wonder, and muddle up the mind
For if the ground didn't reach up to meet my foot
I think I would be fine

Olivia Isabelle Staff
Redlands, CA

Silenced

Do you hear this song?
Listen very closely
The song I sang when I was happy
The beating of drums
As the melody flows
Fast and rapid so as my heart grew

Do you hear the words?
Filled with joy, laughter, hope
A song with sweet melody
That every love-bird knows
Piercing through
The crisp spring air
Touching hearts of those that are near

Listen to this sweet melody
This melody I held dear to me
Now silenced by the ending spring
Just like a passing dream

Lucy Bonny
Irvington, NJ

The Miraculous Ordinary

Embellish for me (if you would) the story of my birth —

Paint my skin blue for countless anxious minutes
Orchestrate the chorus of nurses
The humming of machines
The woodwind of my shallow breath

Sing of my heroic little lungs!

Place us in a foreign land
Soothed by women whose words are strange
So all that's left is an ancient language
Of trust and blood and flesh

Diamond the telling of it
Drown it in sapphires
Place it on the emerald field of adventure

Anything but the ordinary entrance that I made
The miraculous ordinary
One of millions — washed, swaddled, held
But not talked of in the doctors' lounge:

"Remember that one? That tiny girl,
So clearly marked for something special?"

Julie Evan Smith
New York, NY

Julie Evan Smith is a classically trained professional actor as well as an aspiring writer. She holds a MFA from the renowned Old Globe Theatre/University of San Diego graduate program. She has played leading roles at Actors Theatre of Louisville, Dallas Theatre Center, Shakespeare Festival of St. Louis, Great Lakes Theatre Festival and the Old Globe, among others. She also has a "blink and you'll miss it" appearance on an episode of Law & Order *as well as roles in several short films seen by few people other than their directors.*

12:39 A.M.

As I realize the falsity of my
Not blooded family's, dedication and appreciation
My walls cave in
The foundation filled with the rejection
I gave in
Never thinking emotional opportunity could be so
Deceptive
The confusion, turmoil
I can't stress, let alone express it
I never wanted to spread my community
Thinking
I won't make the same mistakes that my mom and dad did
Grant myself immunity
Broke my own laws; sue me
For every crack engraved in my heart
Every good-bye that I let tear myself apart
My heart
Take it in general
Maybe fix it for yourself
Dis-ensemble
Do not be surprised by the complication
Its oblivion
So far ahead, I was
Now I am Mark Twain
'Twas, because
Still
No one will ever see me for what I am internally

Summer Lynn Mathews
Ida Grove, IA

The Forgotten Key

It was quite some time ago that
I chained and locked the door.
Beyond its jam lay memories
I'd rather forget... and more.

I took the key that locks the lock
and tossed it to the sea.
"No one will ever find it.
No one will again hurt me."

The time has lapsed by quickly
No one has bothered the door.
But the changes on the inside
I've never seen before.

"I need not key or crowbar,"
I heard a whisper say,
"for with the stormy weather
the wood has rot away."

"Forget the key that binds you.
The chain has fallen away.
My love's released the darkness
and revealed the light of day."

Janet Vandermey
Minneapolis, MN

Dear Friend,

Jealous of what you have not
Clinging mist, determined to sow rot
With hooked claws to the spine
Venoms refusing the blood clot
With jeweled eyes seeking what I sought —

Though not for comfort like I, no
With visions of glut, you claim all that is mine
Oh treacherous, ravenous crow

In my ears your deprived thoughts churn
In my hands your venoms burn
The heart palpitates, so I dance and shift wills to the beat of thine
On the madness and ash you'll gorge, as the others must wait in turn
This final victory, this punch-line to the first jest, I shan't spurn
But before then, there is something you must learn —

I am grateful, dear friend,
For the laugh is so much sweeter than your cackled caw
For the smile is so much brighter than your menacing maw

Though once more I've found a temporal anodyne
A poison to your poison, a rot to your rot
There will be no punch-line, no final sign for you to dine
So go, Despot of Hope, fly back to your lot —

I'll miss you, dear friend, until your winter comes again.

Dennis Richard Ranahan
Ridgeland, SC

Foggy Mirror

Coating your identity
That isn't mistakable.
That mask cringing at its grasp
Has fused and become so profound to your face.
Hard and cold to touch,
The arch in your brow
The snare of your dismay.

While, metal is encasing,
Holding in deep, harsh, breaths,
Taking over the undertone of your lip,
With every grimacing wink
I feel you stare to rip out my soul,
So that piece missing in your mask will grow
Complete
As you hide behind steel.

I can't break you any more than I can mold you.
Thousands of words
Have shattered, already broken.
I see the pieces missing
So you shelter your inner thoughts with a facial shield.

Reflecting back no solution, no answer
But a faint resemblance of yourself.
Stepping back to try to see it clearer,
Reflected in his mask like a foggy mirror.

Kayla Marie Brewer
Warwick, RI

Mother's Love

You made me whole a place for my soul,
for your love I would never pay a toll.

When I was little you did what you could,
you loved me more than any person would.

When I was hurt you'd say, let me see,
blowing and kissing right there you would be.

When I was bad you had a better way,
but when I was good you would say, *hooray!*

When giving advice it was never a demand,
you were always willing to lend a hand.

When I got older our lives grew apart,
but always together inside our heart.

When time passed by and age set in,
you held me tight like when I was ten.

You did this for me and also my brother,
that's why I love you and call you my mother.

Michael Mick Johnson
Dallas, TX

The Golden Sun Rises and Melts the Snow

The golden sun rises and melts the snow.
The blood of the land reflects in the sky,
But the waves on the beach wash away memories to and fro.

Into the darkness the samurai must go.
The glint of the sword is seen in the eye.
The golden sun rises and melts the snow.

The fire in the heart is the only glow.
Only in the mind do they dare to cry,
But the waves on the beach wash away memories to and fro.

In the tall grass they become hidden by laying low,
Stepping over bodies, on the ground where they lie.
The golden sun rises and melts the snow.

Their fates they will never know,
Fighting in a battle and still do not know why,
But the waves on the beach wash away memories to and fro.

Life and soul they are forced to sew,
With the unnamed graves unable to say good bye.
The golden sun rises and melts the snow,
But the waves on the beach wash away memories to and fro.

Winston Mayo
Marietta, GA

Winston Mayo is a freelance writer, poet and beginner novelist who draws his writing talents from his faith. His is an active Christian who acknowledges the gift God has given him by glorifying Jesus with his works. On his YouTube channel, "The Blessing Report," he showcases spoken word poetry pieces, stand-up comedy performances and honest sermons about having fun as a young adult Christian. He also spends his time making memes on his Instagram page: @the_blessing_report with #theblessingreport. He is currently working on his first novel, Searching for Land. *Currently, he lives in the suburbs of Atlanta in Marietta, GA, but frequently goes to the city. He credits much of writing material to the converging ideologies that make up his thinking: being a male African-American college graduate in his twenties and raised in the South.*

Alone

A candle flickers in the hallway
A figure creeps up the stairs
A floorboard creeks on the landing
The lights go out in pairs

A young girl alone in the bedroom
A dagger to her throat
Her final words "I love you"
As her mind begins to float

A lonely son at a graveyard
Weeping at their graves
His final words "I love you"
As he retreats to the caves

An old man alone in an alley
Lost in his final hours
His final words "I love you"
Then his body surrounded by flowers

Alone and drifting forever
No hope left to find
The darkness overwhelms each one,
Lost lonely minds

Abbie Salkeld
Darlington, County Durham

*I live with my mom, dad and sister Beth. I enjoy art, reading and writing.
I have entered competitions such as the 500 Words BBC Story Contest
where I reached the semi-finals. I enjoy poetry because it's like writing a
story and I enjoy writing stories.*

Mirage

A cold winter day in the afternoon walked on streets of loneliness
Far away in snow was a tall tree with branches but leafless
Two black birds on it exchanged kisses with kindness
Slowly turned and looked into distant past with eagerness
By miracle what I saw was a mirage of illusions so lifeless
Suddenly preferred to continue the journey with forgiveness
Nice starry night reached secretly with silence and darkness
Searched for the moon among shining stars brought happiness
Sometimes choose silence or sometimes smiled with sadness
Complain was a lasting regret unfortunately brought madness
Now the best choice in life is accepting the truth with calmness

Haleh Faryan
Montreal, QC

My poems were published in some anthologies in America. This one, "Mirage," is about my spiritual feeling in life. I got married to Dr. Masoud Moayeri, and we have two children, a son Ali and a daughter Valeh. Both are in their last year of a PhD degree.

Privileged

I found this wounded bird today who needed my loving care.
Her wings that flew her through the heavens,
Were more than she could bear.
So, down to earth she came to me, to restore her health and heart.
How lucky I am to be the one to bring my light into her dark,
To be the one to help her heal and find her strength to fly,
To give her hope and return her to the ever-loving sky.
The tender hold of my embrace will allow her to be unafraid.
The gentle touch I bestow to her, will tell that we are both brave.
So we hold on to each other, so very close and so warm.
She knows I will cover and shelter her from any storm.
We can sit on the window's ledge, and dream of what is to come:
Dreams of the sun kissing her feathers, soaring high above.
I know she will be ready to go, come one day,
But, forever in my heart, she will always stay.
She had nothing to repay me with, nor did I even want to receive,
All I ever wanted were the sweet bird songs she sang to me.

Stacy L. Mata
Bertram, TX

"Privileged" was written about a person who is broken, afraid to trust, and afraid of pain yet finds themselves in the hands of someone willing to care and give them time to realize that they can mend and live again. I am just a simple person who finds comfort in my family and friends. I want everyone to have happiness and peace inside their hearts. My inspiration is found in the normalcy of life, whether I see the colors of the sky, a bird soaring high above or a feeling I get while walking around in the world.

Your Shades

Your smile was a luminous shade of aurous
Glittering in the light that radiated from your body
But that same light cast a shadow over me
My voice becoming disabled in the darkness
No space left for me to bloom or prosper
Like the blushing azaleas in the thawing air

Your lips were a kissable crimson
Just like the crimson lies they conjured up
Because your words were not plush
They were abrasive like aged, rusted nails
Etching into my skin your defaming insults:
Revolting scum
Doltish animal
Nonessential matter

My world once was vibrant in colors
An array of clashing hues
Thriving with maroons and azures
Painting my character across the canvas
But your acidic colors tainted mine
Turning my heart into a burnt shade of ashy coal
Scorched from the years of your condescending aura
That bleeds into my tones and poisons my spirit
My world is now a sullen shade of tenebrous black

Bethany Sanov
High Point, NC

The person who inspired me to continue writing and evolved my love for poetry was Alecia Beymer. With her guidance, I was able to construct pieces of work that convey my inner emotions.

The Time We Didn't Have

There are so many words in this language to say
but when his name is called, there is no right way

He was loved by so many no one could disagree
Why did he have to leave before he met me

There are so many stories, laughs, and cries
The love for him still shines in my father's eyes

Why did he go, why couldn't I meet him
Many people say things happen for a reason

Although it is true, I still don't understand
Why did he go before I got to touch his hands

He left behind a daughter and a wife
He should have had a much longer life

Although I never met him I still could say
He is the best great-grandfather to this day

Valerie Taylor Prazdnik
Fair Lawn, NJ

The Blue Gnu

There was once a blue gnu
Who discovered a shoe.
The blue gnu had a screw
In the sole of his shoe
And the gnu had a slew
Of ewe crew that ate stew.
When the ewe crew construed
To eschew the blue gnu,
The blue gnu had no clue
What to do with his crew.
So he took out the screw
From the sole of his shoe
And screwed the ewe crew for
Inciting a coup.
So now when you see the
Blue gnu with his crew
Know the ewe crew's been screwed with
The blue gnu's shoe's screw.

Angela Skeete-Davis
St. Albans, NY

The Land of Misfit Toys

Did you ever wonder what happens to all of the toys,
That no one gives to any of the world's girls and boys?
The teddy bears smashed at the bottom of the stack
Or the bugs whose antennae were broken with a smack.
Left behind without ever having a chance to fulfill their dream
Of being taken to a place full of warmth and love it would seem.
To receive a child's love was their only reason for being.
Filled with cotton stuffing and glass eyes not for seeing.
So where do they go these misfits from life?
To a place of like kind where there is no strife.
Whenever I find them I try to take as many as I can
To a place that I know, once a cold and gloomy land.
I take them to the land of misfit toys, that is my room,
Once empty and lonely a place for gloom and doom.
Now filled with stuffed animals imperfect yet the love still abounds
To hug me and smile at me as darkness slowly engulfs and surrounds.
No longer alone life's storms to weather,
All of us misfits now banded together.

Sally Jackson
Kenner, LA

Memories of Affection

Blood drew from the burning ember
Etched in my mind is what I remember
A burning flame between two souls
Love played its reckless role
Words spoken softly
Appeared to me as innocent and honest
"I want you forever"
A man's muffled promise
That he will never endeavor
For hours I wept
This too is what I remember
I didn't deserve the anguish and pain
Betray a woman and she'll go outright insane
Now love is nowhere to be found
Like my mother and father who aren't ever around
This too is what I remember

Theresa Rane Little
Watervliet, NY

The Light

The darkness surrounds me,
In the black and the grey,
I've always been alone,
All the lights stay away.

Nothing white, nothing orange,
Has been in my view,
Like my eyelids have been stuck,
Together with glue.

This has been normal,
For weeks after weeks,
Only seeing the black, the grey,
My mind now so bleak.

But then one day I see it,
I see the pale light,
The unfamiliar taste,
But such a beautiful sight.

The light surrounds me,
In the white and the orange,
And now I realize,
For once I'm not alone.

Brianna Ellen O'Callaghan
The Woodlands, TX

The Rhythm of Life

Raindrops tap the windowsill.
Snow geese in flight,
Bluebirds sing in the meadow.
Daffodils delight,
'Tis spring.
Don't let it pass you by.

The fog on the bank, willows bloom,
Walking in the starlight,
Crickets in June,
'Tis summer.
Don't let it pass you by.

Miss seeing you by the oak tree.
Acorns drop, leaves fly by.
Picnic's over. Blackberry pie,
'Tis fall.
Don't let it pass you by.

The pond is frozen over. Snowflakes soar.
Hot chocolate by the fire,
Bears frolic no more.
'Tis winter.
Don't let it pass you by.

Sunshine on the garden gate,
Family from afar,
'Tis spring.
The rhythm of life,
Don't let it pass you by.

Sharon A. Jones
E. Stroudsburg, PA

This poem is written in memory of my mother who passed away February 18, 2015, at the age of eighty-seven.

In Memory of Rod McKuen

A sadness intrudes
on the afternoon,
leaving solitude
trembling in
its own silence.

The eyes of a
beloved poet close
on his life,
feeling like a
blunt nail through
my heart's center.

I raise my head
heavy with grief
to a world of
empathy and loss.

The air chills as
wet snow bleeds
down windowpanes,
across my hollow
heart, like silent
tears of a
mother's mourning.

A bitter taste of
mortality suddenly
rises to my mouth.

Norm Keehn
Thunder Bay, ON

Love Is the Reason

Why does my heart sing?
And I find joy in everything,
Life is so pleasin'
Love is the reason

Why is life so adorable?
Nothing is deplorable,
All my troubles are easin'
Love is the reason

All my friends fill my heart with joy
Every wonderful girl and boy
Why is life so good every season?
Love is the reason

Nothing ever bothers me
My life is so fancy-free
Troubles are never on my mind
Love is the reason I find

Without love the world is a lonely place
Full of hate and disgrace
What makes it all worthwhile
Love is the reason...

R. Bob Hackett
Chatham, ON

Can You Hear It

War is hell!
War is not always our serving.
Do you hear, *the bell?*
It rings far, far, away, away, away,

In foreign land far over the sea,
Where we care but choose not to be.

Our young men's lives cost, too much!
For many *years* we have said *no*,
to such.

How does it happen then?
When will it ever end,
Is it really our mind?

We always bled on land, sea and air.
Once again it is our fare,
To answer everywhere.

Do you hear, *the bell?*

Elenore B. Lowery
Valencia, PA

The Sad Caterpillar

I am a caterpillar and I am sad.
I am not special — my life is bad.
I want to make myself feel good.
I will look for answers in my neighborhood.

If I were a flower I would smell sweet.
I think that life would be really neat.
"Not so," said the flower, "I may be sweet,
But, I cannot move upon my feet."

If I were a bumblebee I could fly
And smell the flowers as I went by.
"Not so," said the bee, "I sure can sway,
But, I must work, I cannot play."

If I were a bird I would be free,
To raise my young up in a tree.
"No so," said the bird, "I sleep in a nest
And that kind of home is not the best."

Then a butterfly came floating by
And said, "Don't be sad and I will try
To explain that you will be just like me
When you grow up, just wait and see."

Not a flower, a bee or even a bird,
Can make me special, or so I've heard.
I need to grow up and there might be
A chance for me to be happy.

Susan Francis
North York, ON

Sky High

why get yourself in so deep
when all they ever do is leave

why do people hold onto the temporary
everything will change by next January

life love
it all goes away
everyone, everything
leaves, they never stay
even the moon, sun, stars slowly give way

is the pain in the end worth it all
is love worth the foreshadowed fall

is the heaven worth the hell
why not live untouchable
not lovable

just getting by
floating on the clouds
drifting in the sky
not living deep

living high

Annabelle Louise Ahlers
Oconomowoc, WI

Return to Dust

I saw you again on the train platform.

Your coat was pulled tightly around your body to keep out the cold.
Or maybe to trap it in.
Your lips are pursed around the end of a cigarette,
pulling in the warm smoke and letting it free again.
I watch it fill the air, food coloring dripped into a glass of water.

Your eyes track passengers and train cars as they move to and fro.

Where are they headed?
Exeter to San Francisco?
Burlington to Cambridge?
Some go farther than that, to places that have never been seen.

The tracks carve lines on the face of the earth, signs of age.
You however, don't.
You stay young, stay sad.
The barren landscape of your heart
is dotted with abandonment and dead brush.
The trains you ride run horizon to horizon,
over the dateline and back through time.

How much longer can you keep this up?
How much longer before your body gives out
and the age catches up all at once...

...and you return to dust.

Nicholas Eshbaugh
Fayetteville, NY

The Man with the Beat

Willie and Waylon, you're the greatest I know,
but where would you be if not for those backup boys.
They're behind you all of the time,
keeping the beat while you sing out your rhymes.
The man with the beat.
A great bunch of guys with unusual names,
but their music and talent puts the rest to shame.
The heavenly music of an angel's harp
echoes from some old beat up guitar.
The soft sound like satin and lace
flows from an electric bass.
Old Mezz himself has musical hands,
he writes the music and adds to the greatness of this band.
The man with the beat.
Chimes, drum roll, or thunder sounds,
he will give you a beat that will make you really get down.
No band is ever complete,
unless you have "a man with the beat."
Forever in Heaven may your drums be heard,
while the angels keep your beat,
as they dance upon golden streets.
May you never be outdone.
Thank you, God, for this drummer is my son.

Peggy Atwood
Pampa, TX

*This poem was written for my oldest son, Kendall Mesneak. I am so very
proud of him and I love him as much as possible with all of my heart.*

God's Portrait

Lord, if I asked would you paint a portrait of me today?
What would you ask of me?
Might you paint me a guardian angel to help another soul
like me, or maybe you could help ease another's pain
through me?
Send me to fill a room with laughter and help others not to
stray. Sing your praise and guide someone through each
and every day.
Erase the hurt in someone's eyes, touch them all with
humble sighs.
If you would paint me Lord, in whose eyes would I see, in
whose heart would I feel, whose life would I touch?
Could I walk others through their darkest hours,
caress a rose along the way, or feel the pain in someone's
heart each and every day?
Oh Lord, where would I be, if you painted me today?

Jean Ritter
Wyoming, PA

Untitled

A dog is called "man's best friend."
He will play ball until day's end,
or go hunting with people for deer and fowl,
kill snakes and mice and coyotes that howl.

They are heroes in many ways.
In a blizzard one carried medicine for days
to a place in Alaska
that is far away.

One dog rescued forty people lost in snow.
One flew over the North Pole
when it was sixty below.
Another was the first space traveler to go.

Dogs entertain people at movies and races.
We're always surprised at how fast their pace is.
In a circus they do many kinds of tricks,
roll a barrel and jump over sticks.

Sometimes dogs are smarter than we are.
When I was a child ours heard thunder from afar,
before we could see storms in the sky.
He would be frightened and begin to cry.

Helma Lein
Dickinson, ND

The Longest Winter Ever

The longest winter ever
Snowed in October
Stayed on through March
Ran out of things to talk about
Got sick of hearing you reminisce about old times
Too sick to make anything new happen
Watching us grow old
Pains in our bodies
Regret on our breath
The longest winter ever

Dawn Duane
Kalispell, MT

Black Privilege

I have the privilege of being profiled, wherever I go,
because perpetuated stereotypes are hard to forgo.
No father, because of mass incarceration.
Profiling to cops, is easier than an open investigation.
My history is not being taught in schools.
I, raped and stolen, just to be used as tools.
Masters were able to evolve, allowing theirs the very best.
As a colored-American
would you be happy with the rest?

Samantha Clementina Holmes
Albany, NY

Love

Love is like no other,
And you love it near and dear!
But sometimes when you're not watching,
It will come and bite you in the rear.

But love will take you everywhere,
And bring you to places you have never been,
To meet the love you need to have,
'Cause love will always win.

When you throw things away,
Love will always bring them back,
'Cause love always loves you,
And always has your back.

When you don't have enough energy,
To keep going on,
Love will make you happy,
And keep you going,
Forever on and on.

Elli Karemy MacDonald
Anderson, SC

My name is Ellianna, and I live in South Carolina with my parents and two brothers. I attend the Montessori School of Anderson, and I am in the sixth grade. I wrote this poem in fourth grade during our study of poetry. Mrs. Coffey is my wonderful poetry teacher who has taught me so much. When she asked our class to write a poem, I thought about love, and so that is what I wrote about.

Cold Wooden Seats

Defined by a number
Becoming a statistic
A place with so much pressure
Just struggling to be optimistic
They say the only important thing is to get a degree
But what happened to letting our minds and hearts roam free?
The Pythagorean theorem has zero impact on any life choice
But at least my poetry has given me a voice
Being taught things we'll never use again
We should be taught art, love, creativity and equality of men
They say if you follow your heart and don't do the normal way
You'll become a bum
The only way to succeed is to follow their narrow-minded curriculum
Along the way we lose our identities
Because the only path there is, is the path they want us to see
Expected to act like adults
Setting the wrong tone
Considering the fact we make no decisions on our own
Taught that money defines success
Even though true success is based on the love in your chest
Took away our creativity, took away our voice
Took away our minds to be free
Now sit down, stop talking and close your imagination
In those cold wooden seats

Michael Salvatore Affatato
Naperville, IL

Index of Poets

A

Abbate, Donna Marie 202
Acheson, Jaylene 272
Adzema, Elizabeth Michelle 155
Affatato, Michael Salvatore 303
Ahlers, Annabelle Louise 296
Ahmad, Ramadhan 166
Allawala, Aamnah Mansoor 154
Allen, Betty L. 109
Al-Moamen, Amen J. 32
Amburgey, Rachel Kaye 267
Amundsen, Sarah Elizabeth 210
Armentrout, Christy 244
Atwood, Peggy 298
Atwood, Sherman 58
Austin, Jody-lynne Nicole 149
Avenido, Tricia 74

B

Baboo, Dorothy 241
Badiable, Le 71
Bagley, Paul Ethan 161
Bagnato, Carmela A. 74
Baker, Shyanne 86
Bangerter, Jerald Christian 99
Barga Napier, Karin 78
Batov, Phillip 129
Beaty, Cameron Joseph 77
Bennett, Patty Perreault 108
Bennett, Rejena 240
Bennington, Chandra C. 128
Benson, Tujuanna 242
Berggren, Hannah Rose 133
Berk, Adam 193
Bessette, Michelle 227
Bianco, Olivia Yvonne 203
Bitzer, Brian Thomas 18
Boling, Howard 11
Bonny, Lucy 274

Bratton, Amber 19
Brause, Joanne 78
Brewer, Kayla Marie 279
Brewster, Marilyn Nellie G. 256
Brown, Clare 156
Bryant, Emily Rose 194
Buckland, Cassidy 214
Buffum, Angelique Ann Marie 249
Bunting, Amy 126
Burky, Seth 168

C

Campbell Leonard, Lanalee J. 232
Cannon, Kody Lee 102
Cantwell, Thomas 253
Carey, Ninette 98
Carico, Grace Ryanne 169
Carlson, Eric 58
Carter, Maggie Mae 29
Casler, Janice Theresa 117
Chappell, Erin Elizabeth 172
Chegwin, Emily Lindsey 79
Chimenti, Alex 61
Chung, Joyce 142
Clardy, Raymond 206
Clayton, Walter E. 233
Coberley, Ann 73
Cohen, Alexa 165
Coker, Kayleigh Brianna 16
Colin, Victor Josue 27
Collins, Sonja Mapuana A. 48
Connor, Ryan 53
Corrigan, Florence 141
Cortez, Cristina 187
Coudriet, Morgan C. 135
Coulter, Angela Dawn 23

D

Dague, Adam 180
Darks, Taylor Bianca 254
Davis, Hannah Marie 266
Dawidian, Sara 112
Dayjr, Marshall Neal 184
DeConte, Claire 60
Devulyte, Nevis 5
Diffenderfer, Erin 185
DiMartino, Dawn M. 85
Dinov, Victoria 35
Dresner, Hannah 146
Duane, Dawn 301
Duffield, Laura 197
Dunn, Ella Chapman 153
Dunn, Nancy Ann 218
Durham, Maya 235

E

Eagle, Kaitlyn Jayne 104
Edelman, Cathryn 14
Elder-Clark, Brianna 148
Elder, Isabel 121
Elqasass, Basil M. 211
Eoppolo, Benita 33
Eshbaugh, Nicholas 297
Eskridge, Paulene 83
Evans, Abby D. 190
Ewald, Lauren Ellyse 250
Ewy, Hailey 171

F

Faryan, Haleh 283
Fleetwood, Ashley Cohagan 95
Floren, Ben 173
Francis, Susan 295
Friedson, Brittany 89
Furtado, Lisa Marie Roy 102

G

Garner, Randle Stinson 38
George, Corey Dean 158
Giambanco, Shannon Marie 9
Giardina, Sarah 136
Gilbow, Glen W. 1
Goldeman, Sydney 177
Gordon, Carol 121
Graham, Rhonda 189
Groak, Stephen John 182
Guerard, Patricia 119
Guisao, Jason 175

H

Hackett, R. Bob 293
Hall, Alison Grace 248
Hall, Jeff 220
Hall, Judith J. 224
Hall, Karen T. 243
Hamilton, Hailie Michelle 67
Hamilton, Katherine Elise 204
Hammond, Mariah 158
Hancock, William Lee 236
Hanson, Gavin James Edward 76
Harry, Karsyn 45
Hawkins, Ross A. 230
Henley, James Marion 47
Hill, Teresa Victoria 181
Holmes, Samantha C. 301
Hosford, Colleen Lear 39
Houk, Jackie 28
Howe, Shawn 164
Hurd, Kathleena Mercedes 118
Hyler, James, II 178

I

Iqbal, Noor 12

J

Jackson, Sally 288
James, Lena Suzanne 95

James, Stephen 123
Jean-Baptiste, Gregory 144
Jenkins, Jamie C. 262
Jenkins, Josephine 223
Johnson, Michael Mick 280
Jones, Hanna Marie 196
Jones, Lonnie, Jr. 213
Jones, Maryn Margaret 212
Jones, Michael Jason 25
Jones, Samantha 237
Jones, Sharon A. 291

K

Kamazima, Oscar 10
Kaye, Adriana 174
Kaye, Robert V. 82
Kearsch, Dixie Rose 188
Keehn, Norm 292
Kelly, Samantha Lynn 167
Keyser, Kelly 132
Kim, Jenny 260
Kim, Yuna 34
King, Ralph 226
Kiusals, Julia 231
Klein, Linda 96
Koloske, Keith 145
Konstantino, Kadeelyn Nicole 147
Kozlowski, Tom 15
Kruchinski, Travis 110

L

Lafever, Creighton 195
Lalumondier, Anna 162
Larson, Evan 113
Law, Kurell 120
Lech, Tom, Jr. 116
Ledesma, Aliah G. 65
Lein, Helma 300
Lesko, John 98
Lightle, Carlee Ann 186
Little, Theresa Rane 289
Livdahl, Alice Klippel 130
Looney, Alexandra Ruth 17

Lorenzo, Janet 62
Lowery, Elenore B. 294
Luckey, Shawna Ree 112
Lynch, Aress 216
Lyndon, Kyrian 52

M

MacDonald, Elli Karemy 302
Madill, Michael 114
Magby, Theresa 116
Majewski, Michael 221
Mangum, Ladise 3
Mara, Danny 43
Mariage, Brenden 180
Martin, William 76
Martzen, Barbara A. 255
Mata, Stacy L. 284
Mathews, Summer Lynn 276
Matteis, Matthew 131
Maye, Shyanne 93
Mayo, Winston 281
McAleer, Deborah Curlew 238
McGrann, John Vincent, III 124
McKee, Marissa Kailey 50
McKee, Nina M. 13
McNeel, KarLee 246
Mendez, Ruth 8
Menear, Kenneth Lee 177
Metz, Melissa R. 53
Meyerzon, Mark 179
Meyong Krishack, Celine 92
Middleton, Amy 69
Miller, Brenda Kay 103
Miller, Joshua 80
Miller, Julliet Ann-Marie 122
Miller, Kimberly 36
Mohnike, Kerry 87
Moore, Sarai 41
Moran, Michele Lauren 263
Morris, Jay 208
Morrissey, Spencer George 83
Mosier-McHenry, Candace Jean 7
Munir, Aisha 200
Murray, Erin 219

N

Nader, Beverly 225
Neeley, Jennifer Jane 42
Nelson, Jessica 127
Nepomnyashchiy, Mikhail 157
Nichols, Pat 160
Nidadavolu, Chitra Amba 258
Noire, Angelique 269
Norman, Juliet Paige 104

O

O'Callaghan, Brianna Ellen 290
Occiahlini, Ava 140
Ortiz, Samuel Kane, III 228

P

Parent, Lian Thomas 191
Parks, Ruby M. 94
Pellegrom, Margaret Vivian 268
Perez, Alicia 24
Perna, Tina L. 259
Petnuch, Nicolette 170
Pichardo, Emmitt Joseph 125
Piercy, Christina Lynn 37
Pierre, Terese Mason 255
Pipes, Kate E. 148
Polanco, Paola Izamar 126
Pollihan, Madison 63
Porter, Yolanda W. 257
Potter, Heather 46
Prakhina, Leena 101
Prazdnik, Valerie Taylor 286
Proa, Teresa Xochitl V. 201
Purcell, Jeffrey A. 30
Purfield, Amanda Hayley 75

R

Ranahan, Dennis Richard 278
Ranchod, Atul 72
Randazzo, Anthony 209

Rand, Ronald 138
Recker, Marisa J. 261
Revilla, Joan Elizabeth 20
Rice, Rachael Lee 265
Richardson, Drake Dudley 252
Rieser, Patrick Louis 154
Ritter, James B. 2
Ritter, Jean 299
Roberts, Chessie 128
Roberts, Vonda and Bud 222
Rocca, Naomi 251
Rockwell, Cindi Griggs 247
Rodriguez, Ariel Ana 54
Rodriguez, Raidys 68
Roetter, Dovid Nissan 106
Rosenberg, Tehilla 146
Roychowdhury, Mitra 198
Rubertone, Kristina Téa 143
Ruzbacki, Serena 127
Ryan, Lindsey 270
Rychagov, Nicole Victoria 150

S

Sahota, Simran Kaur 66
Salazar, Natalye Michelle 6
Salkeld, Abbie 282
Sammartino, Dayna 159
Sanov, Bethany 285
Santiago, Natalie E. 8
Scaife, Natasha Lynne 22
Scott, Kinsey Rebecca 64
Segura, Kathleen E. M. 21
Shamiya, Claire 152
Shi, Andrew 4
Shorr, Dave 178
Shute, Carol 239
Sick, Morgan 99
Sims, Maggie 97
Sisson, Danielle Blakley 81
Skeete-Davis, Angela 287
Skoczen, Jeniffer 31
Smith, Jacob 216
Smith, Julie Evan 275
Spainhower, Anita M. 55
Staff, Olivia Isabelle 273

Stauffer, Kimberley Martin 100
Stayton, Carol Holekamp 40
Stotts, Ronald Taylor 183
Stull, Theresa 9
Sullivan, Jill Marie 151
Swanson, Barbara 234
Sweet, Courtney 137

T

Tahtinen, Jennifer 163
Tally, Corabelle 70
Taubinger, Hope 176
Taylor, Warren E. 105
Teichner, Nicole 199
Thomas, Floyd J. 217
Thomas, Selena Shandi 90
Thompson, Kathleen 84
Tilton, Glendell 229
Toal, Lisa Marie 134
Turner, Meredith Drake 44
Tuvell, Meagan Elaine 207

U

Ulrich, Robert Hadley 91

V

Vandermey, Janet 277
Vandieren, Lindsey Jae 270
Van Ekeren, Nikki Lena 59
Vargo, Ashley Breann 215
Vazquez, Tiara 49
Velez, Samantha 234
Viswanadha, Sravani 264

W

Wagley, Jim Frank 107
Wallace, Morgan 111
Wall, Jennifer 57
White, Katie E. 115
Williams, Corrissa 245

Williams, Rachal 56
Williams, Samantha 205
Wilson, Alexander Nikolai 26
Wright, Lorenzo 51

Y

Yeates, Lynda C. 88
Yoder, Christian M. 139
Yodhhewawhe, Yehuwdiyth 192

Z

Zinn, Katya Melissa 271